"A practical and insightful guide to quality transformation. Sumeet explains the theoretical and practical considerations of leading large scale change, involving stakeholders and linking strategy from the front line to the board table."
—**Paul Heinrich**, President and CEO, North Bay Regional Health Centre

"A thought-provoking book that provides leaders a structure to subjective nuances of creating an organizational culture. Sumeet will walk you through a journey of self-realization and courage; the courage it takes to transform your leadership and the organization."
—**Stéphane Giguère**, CEO, Ottawa Community Housing Corporation

"A management-excellence playbook for business leaders to be successful in this world of constant change. This book provides the tools necessary to guide the change journey from the beginning when defining your Change Vision, through the middle when ensuring Employee Engagement, to the end, when confirming the change sticks."
—**Corina Moore**, President and CEO, Ontario Northland

"A brilliant interplay of Lean Management and Leadership Courage. Sumeet takes the reader on an exciting journey of excellence filled with teachable moments. A required reading for all leaders."
—**Marc Gauthier**, Director of Education, CSPGNO

"In today's lightning fast paced global economy, those that strive for advantages long before most recognize a challenge, will be the leaders of today and the future. This book is an accelerator for those they truly want to be at the top of their game."
—**Mayor Al McDonald**, City of North Bay

"An excellent resource for leaders embarking on a culture transformation journey. Sumeet provides the reader with a systematic approach supported with real case examples of leading behavior change in an organization. The pictorial representation of technical concepts, models and tools makes the book more interesting, provides clarity to visual folks, and enhances reader's learning experience."
—**Nancy H. Jacko**, former Vice President and Chief Nursing Executive, NBRHC

"This book is a valuable resource explaining the various types of change along with key strategies to ensure success. The emphasis on change behaviors at the leadership and staff levels for organization transformation is paramount. What a terrific synthesis of management excellence. A must-have manual for leaders!"
—**Joanne Bezzubetz**, Vice President Patient Care Services, The Royal Ottawa Mental Health Centre

"Sumeet takes a principles based approach to leading sustainable change. Blending theories and actual experience, the book provides the reader with practical tools for organizational quality transformation."
—**Dr. Susan J. Adams**, former Chief of Psychiatry, NBRHC

T0371682

Courageous Leadership
The Missing Link to Creating
a Lean Culture of Excellence

Courageous Leadership

The Missing Link to Creating
a Lean Culture of Excellence

Sumeet Kumar

Routledge
Taylor & Francis Group

A PRODUCTIVITY PRESS BOOK

First published 2018
by Routledge
2 Park Square, Milton Park, Abingdon, Oxon OX14 4RN

and by Routledge
711 Third Avenue, New York, NY 10017

Routledge is an imprint of the Taylor & Francis Group, an informa business

British Library Cataloguing-in-Publication Data
A catalogue record for this book is available from the British Library

ISBN: 978-1-138-10439-6 (hbk)
ISBN: 978-1-138-10438-9 (pbk)
ISBN: 978-1-315-10225-2 (ebk)

Typeset in ITC Garamond Std Light
by Nova Techset Private Limited, Bengaluru & Chennai, India

Contents

List of Figures

List of Tables

Preface

Bernard Baruch once said, "If all you have is a hammer, everything looks like a nail." Likewise, "transformation" has become a buzzword today. It is unfortunate that it is being misused and overmarketed through books, articles, conferences, and other media. It is often substituted incorrectly to represent any small or incremental change in the performance of any process, product, or service. Specific process-improvement tools and methodologies that are best suited for incremental and transitional change are promoted as silver bullets for a transformational change. This has led to a lot of confusion and frustration in the minds of business leaders, practitioners, staff, and other professionals as they struggle to implement these tools and methodologies in their organizations but fail to achieve the results of transformation.

At the same time, the role of courage in leadership has often been underplayed in a transformational journey. Most literature on change management and transformation mentions the importance of stakeholder engagement, senior management commitment, and leadership buy-in, but fails to recognize courage as a key attribute of leaders when the odds to succeed are high.

As a practitioner of business excellence for more than 20 years, I wrote this book, which is one of the first of its kind, to wade through the confusion among leaders on selecting the type of change approach that will get the best results in their organization and how the approach to transformational change is different from incremental and transitional change. Senior leaders and practitioners will benefit the most from reading this book as I share my experiences from leading several small- and large-scale organization transformations in multiple industries across different countries. I explain how to establish a robust foundation for a journey toward excellence and to integrate strategy into daily operations. Also, I discuss what it means to be a courageous leader while overseeing change in difficult situations and what leaders do differently to put their organization on a path to excellence and cultural transformation.

In this book, I have shared a few custom-designed models and frameworks implemented at a hospital in Canada, which propelled the organization further ahead in their transformational journey compared to other organizations that started much earlier. The innovative model combined best practices and principles from Malcolm Baldrige, Shingo, Lean, Six Sigma, Balanced Scorecard, accreditation, change management, patient and family-centered care, the Competing Values Framework, the LEADS framework, and the project management body of knowledge.

It has been my endeavor that the book serves as a practical guide and not a cookbook for senior executive leaders and organizational excellence practitioners, who wish to embark on or are in various stages of their journey toward organizational excellence and cultural transformation. Readers will be guided through 26 elements necessary for establishing a robust foundation and an additional set of 22 management system elements required to create and sustain a culture of quality across the organization. For leaders in healthcare, I have put together a framework to support the implementation of the four core concepts of patient and family-centered care, namely, dignity and respect, information sharing, participation, and collaboration. In addition, I have included several examples with creative visuals and ready-to-use templates, as well as standard works, models, guiding principles, and strategies that are based on best practices to assist you in your transformational journey.

Sensei in Japanese means "teacher" and *gyaan* in Sanskrit means "knowledge." Brief notes labeled "Sensei Gyaan" have been interspersed throughout the book to provide valuable tips to the reader based on my experiential learning over the past two decades. When people ask me what I do, I tell them "whatever it takes." All my life I have worked as a porter— portering and transferring knowledge from one area to another, from one department to another, from one organization to another, from one industry to another, from one hospital to another, from one province to another, and from one country to another. This is what I have done all my life and I am passionate about what I do as a porter. The pace and approach changed from one implementation to another, depending upon how soon the organization needed to see the results of transformation.

Remember, there is only one way to learn. It's through action. Franklin D. Roosevelt said, "There are many ways of going forward but only one way of standing still." In the animated movie, "The Hunchback of Notre Dame," the character Laverne says to Quasi, "Life's not a spectator sport. If watchin' is all you're gonna do, then you're gonna watch your life go by without ya."

My humble submission to all readers is to employ six honest serving-men like Rudyard Kipling did—*What, Why, When, How, Where, and Who.* They will teach you all you need to know. And dare to have courage. Sometimes the smallest step in the right direction ends up as a biggest step of your life. Tip toe if you must, but take the step.

Happy learning!

Sumeet Kumar

Acknowledgements

All models, templates, methodologies, and strategies presented in this book have been tested and applied in real organizations. I have invented some of them, and I have adapted and improved many of them. I have combined them in creative ways to suit the specific circumstances of complex organizations. The content of this book has evolved over more than 20 years of experimenting and learning at different organizations that I worked with or consulted for. It has been influenced by every business I have worked with and every book and article that I have read. I do most sincerely thank all of them. This book, however, is my own paradigm and any limitations or errors that it may contain are my own. In the same breath, I would like to reiterate the words of Joel Barker: "The future is very important. It is where we will spend the rest of our lives. The success of the past does not guarantee the success for the future. Once the paradigm shifts, everyone goes back to zero."

Among many others, I would like to especially thank

- Wendy Degagne for translating my technical knowledge into easy-to-understand creative visuals and for remaining a true friend;
- my business partners Natalie Lepine and Micheline Demers for sharing a common passion to drive excellence at client organizations;
- Dr. Dean Anderson, Dr. Linda Ackerman Anderson, and Marcella Bremer for supporting the community of change agents through their blogs, articles, books, and other superior quality literature on leading change and culture transformation at organizations; and
- my wife Puja along with my two lovely daughters, Aarushi and Aarohi, for sacrificing their family time while I completed this book.

Author

With broad experience spanning two decades, Sumeet Kumar has been leading individuals and organizations through business and cultural transformation. He has a proven track record for stimulating organic business growth, increasing revenues and profits, and decreasing overhead.

Organizational excellence through strategy planning and execution, innovation, continuous quality improvement, and project management has been the focus of his partnerships with boards as well as leadership and executive teams in the automotive, food, chemical, paper, textile, education, social housing, and healthcare industries. Sumeet has expertise in optimizing systems and processes, along with improving and developing integrated quality, risk, safety, and management system frameworks that complement departmental and enterprise-wide policies.

A mechanical engineer with an MBA, he has held a number of titles that speak to his expertise in strategic systemic change, including vice president and business head, chief strategy officer, director of transformation, and quality deployment leader, among others. A certified project management professional, a Black Belt in Lean Six Sigma, and a Master Black Belt in Innovation, he is an expert motivator who brings an infectious enthusiasm to every change initiative. In Canada, he is one of only three consultants trained to conduct the organizational culture assessment instrument (OCAI).

Sumeet's professional reputation and passion for driving positive culture change by integrating best practices and principles of Malcolm Baldrige, Shingo, Accreditation, ISO, GMP, Six Sigma, TQM, TPM, WCM, and Lean quality management into daily operations has made him a sought-after speaker at national and international forums. In 2015, he founded KFI

Management Consulting (www.kumarfriends.com), which provides advisory services to clients in the areas of designing and implementing Lean management system frameworks, strategy planning and execution, and building capacity in organizations to support operational and cultural transformation.

An adventurous soul and dedicated family man, he loves to travel. He enjoys swimming and a vigorous game of badminton. He can be reached at sumeet@kumarfriends.com.

Introduction

Are you more concerned about the quality of your business or are you concentrating more on getting deeper into the business of quality?

—Mikel J. Harry

For a long time, businesses worldwide have been leveraging best practices, principles, and methodologies to improve their performance. An overview of the evolution of quality to support organizational excellence and culture transformation is presented in Figure I.1. The diagram provides timelines when certain methodologies and best practices first gained acceptance within different industries. With new knowledge and applications, some of these methodologies have evolved over time to keep pace with unprecedented change and still remain relevant to the industry, while others have either been phased out or used less frequently.

Over the years, many industries have created regulatory standards specific to their own industry. All organizations within that industry are required to comply with them to ensure that the basic quality of the product and/or service received by the consumer is standard across different organizations. Unfortunately, meeting and complying with these standards does not provide an organization a competitive edge to differentiate themselves in the market place. Therefore, forward thinking organizations undertake competitive benchmarking and explore other best practices and methodologies to improve their business performance. With so many different methodologies, models, approaches, and standards available to choose from, it has become extremely challenging for both senior executive leaders and business excellence practitioners to select the ones that are most appropriate for getting the results that they need.

Further, the literature informs that 70% of transformation programs and 54% of process improvement projects fail. The fear of failure ties our hands

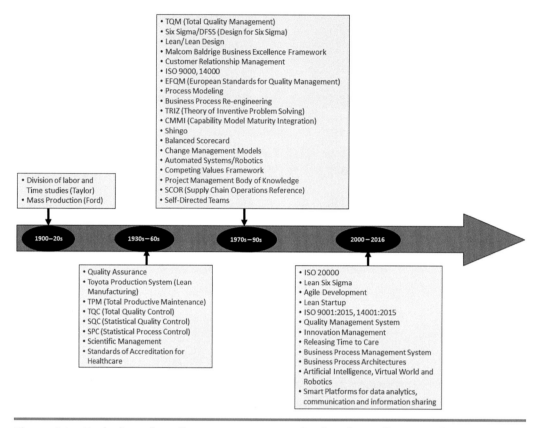

Figure I.1 Evolution of quality to support organizational excellence and cultural transformation.

against taking calculated risks and moving forward at the pace required for a business to turn around and survive. Eighty-seven percent of the Fortune 500 companies that existed in 1955 are no longer on the same list today. Some went bankrupt, some merged and some fell from grace. Many lost their way or failed to keep up with the times, and faded away. The average lifespan of a company listed on the S&P 500 has decreased from sixty-seven years in the 1920s to fifteen years today. Overall, 40% of the S&P companies that exist today won't exist in the next ten years.

The advantage you have yesterday, will be replaced by the trends of tomorrow. You don't have to do anything wrong, as long as your competitors catch the wave and do it RIGHT, you can lose out and fail.

To change and improve yourself is giving yourself a second chance. To be forced by others to change, is like being discarded. Those who refuse to learn and improve, will definitely one day become redundant and not relevant to the industry. They will learn the lesson in a hard and expensive way.

To avoid becoming a statistic, it becomes important to address some fundamental questions: What are the criteria for selecting an appropriate methodology and to decide when one methodology should be considered over the other? What are the similarities and differences between the characteristics of different change types? Can one methodology handle all the different types of change that organizations desire? How do you manage different types of change? What behavioral attributes are required from leaders? There are many more. If these questions are not thought through before or during a change journey, the organization can be driven along the wrong path, which leads to frustration and anxiety in teams, thereby causing low employee morale and trust in the excellence journey.

Practitioners have realized that no methodology is self-sufficient to deliver the best results by itself (even though some claim to be all encompassing) and each has its own pros and cons. While some are good at addressing efficiency and effectiveness issues, others are good at managing behavioral change in an organization. Also, since most methodologies complement each other, practitioners have started to combine principles and best practices from various methodologies to create frameworks that are customized to meet the needs of that organization.

In the 26 chapters of the book, you will be privy to a few customized models and frameworks that were instrumental in transforming Hospital Heal in Canada (the name has been changed to protect the hospital's identity). These models and frameworks combine best practices and principles from Malcolm Baldrige, Shingo, Balanced Scorecard, Lean, Six Sigma, accreditation, change management, patient and family-centered care, the Competing Values Framework, the LEADS framework, and the project management body of knowledge. Section F focuses on the leadership trait of courage and the types of courage that leaders demonstrate in an organizational journey of transformation.

The approach and the strategies explained across the six parts of this book will guide senior leaders and practitioners who wish to fast-track their organization on a path to excellence and cultural transformation on the twenty-six elements that are critical for establishing a robust foundation in a transformational journey, along with an additional set of twenty-two management system elements required to create and sustain a culture of quality across the organization. The frameworks shared in this book improve the richness of the best practice models available to implement change that engages the frontline to increase overall performance and to deliver on an organization's strategic plan.

CREATE A
SHARED NEED

Chapter 1

Understand the Need for Change

The only thing of real importance that leaders do is to create and manage culture. If you do not manage culture, it manages you, and you may not even be aware of the extent to which this is happening.

—Edgar Schein

Recognizing the need for change must be established before undertaking any excellence journey. There has to be an inspiring reason (not a burning platform) that creates a desire to initiate change in an organization. Burning platforms are helpful while running a sprint, not a marathon. A transformational journey undertaken purely on the basis of a burning platform has a very narrow internal focus. It creates an environment of uncertainty where employees fear job loss; protect their own interest; construe management as the enemy; and feel helpless, disengaged, and demotivated.

Are You Too Busy to Improve?

On the other hand, a need based on a meaningful purpose, expected to positively impact customer, patient, or social outcomes, has a broad external focus. When reinforced and communicated extensively, this need draws much higher commitment. It inspires people to share a common vision, take personal accountability to change behavior, and hold one another responsible—all ingredients in a successful transformation.

If you are not sure about the nature of your need, it is advisable you conduct an assessment to guide your decision making. Some of the assessments, among many others, include the following:

1. Readiness for change assessment
2. Operational assessment
3. Growth assessment
4. Customer/patient/partner experience assessments
5. External environmental scan
6. Strategy assessment
7. Organizational culture assessment
8. Organizational health check

To assist leaders and practitioners in selecting the type of assessment that would be most meaningful to their organization, I created Figure 1.1, which leverages learning from the Competing Values Framework. Let me first provide you an overview of this framework.

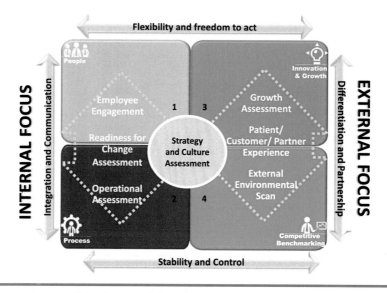

Figure 1.1 **Understanding the need for change using the Competing Values Framework.**

The Competing Values Framework (CVF) was developed initially from research conducted by University of Michigan faculty members on the major indicators of effective organizational performance. It has been found to be an extremely useful model for organizing and understanding a wide variety of organizational and individual phenomena, including theories of organizational effectiveness, leadership competencies, organizational culture, organizational design, stages of life-cycle development, organizational quality, leadership roles, financial strategy, information processing, and brain functioning. The robustness of the framework is one of its greatest strengths. In fact, the framework has been identified as one of the forty most important frameworks in the history of business.

The Competing Values Framework explains that every organization is a mix of four culture types, namely, people, process, innovation and growth, and competitive benchmarking. Industries or organizations that are heavily dependent on their people, processes, and existing products/services to increase organizational performance have a more internal focus. Their strategy to optimize processes and resources is through integration and their emphasis is on improving bottom-line results. On the other hand, industries or organizations that choose to be innovative and competitive in the marketplace, to strategically differentiate themselves through new products and services, and to establish partnerships to delight their customers are externally focused. They base their performance on growing the top line.

That said, what was true for an industry to operate in a certain manner in the past is shifting dramatically to keep pace with unprecedented change. The healthcare and education industries have traditionally been more provider focused, when it was acceptable for the care providers and educators to decide on behalf of their patients and students, respectively, what was good for them. Over a period of time, however, with easier access to technology and information; increased competition in the marketplace; and availability of services that are faster, better, and cheaper, patients and students have become more educated and informed. They have wider choices. This has contributed to a shift in decision-making power to the patients, students, and their families. It has forced the healthcare and education industries to provide services that are more patient and student centered and to continuously improve their offerings to meet the constantly increasing expectations of their customers.

I would encourage leaders and practitioners to keep this framework in mind and undertake assessments that will help them in identifying gaps and designing strategies to move closer to the vision of their organization. Also, when the organization is considering an operational excellence journey, it is advisable to conduct a readiness assessment and evaluate the culture of the organization. A good instrument for measuring the current state and for developing the desired future state of your organization's culture is the Organization Cultural Assessment Instrument (OCAI). It is a validated instrument based on CVF that has been extensively used in many industries across the globe. It is easy to understand, relate, and administer, and a discussion of the quantitative results of the survey engages people at all levels to agree on a shared vision.

Business and Culture

Senior leadership teams spend countless hours on strategy planning and execution, implementing Lean, carrying out project management, and undertaking team-building activities, but they are still unable to get the desired results.

Research has identified that what differentiates a top-performing organization from others is their "culture," an unseen force that not only drives organizational excellence but also sustains transformational change.

The 2017 PEX Network's, "Global State of Process Excellence" report indicates that the number one area for an organization to focus in 2018–2019 will be leadership and culture strategy, followed by process redesign work, customer-centric process management, change management strategy, and process automation.

According to a 2015 global survey conducted by Korn Ferry,

- "Driving culture change" ranks among the top three global leadership development priorities.
- "Organizational alignment and collaboration" is considered the primary driver to improve culture.
- "Communications" is the most used strategy to improve culture, followed by "leadership development" and "embedding culture change in management objectives."

Culture change occurs, ultimately, when a critical mass of individuals adopt new behaviors consistent with their organization's strategic direction.

The above results are not very different from a previous study conducted by Booz & Company (now PricewaterhouseCoopers), in November 2013 (Figure 1.2).

Even the 2016 McKinsey digital survey of global executives identified shortcomings in organizational culture as one of the main barriers to company success in the digital age. Julie Goran, Laura LaBerge, and Ramesh Srinivasan in their article "Culture for a Digital Age," published in the July 2017 *McKinsey Quarterly*, mention that the executives who wait for organizational cultures to change organically will move too slowly as digital penetration grows, blurs the boundaries between sectors, and boosts competitive intensity. They further highlight that executives must be proactive in shaping and measuring culture, approaching it with the same rigor and discipline with which they tackle operational transformations. This includes changing structural and tactical elements in an organization that run counter to the culture change the organization is trying to achieve.

Psychologists George Litwin, Richard Stringer, and David McClelland refer to six key factors that influence an organization's working environment (climate) and therefore its culture: its *flexibility*—that is, how free employees feel to innovate unencumbered by red tape; their sense of *responsibility* to the organization; the level of *standards* that people set; the sense of accuracy about

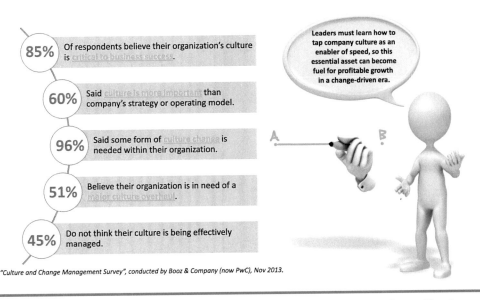

85% Of respondents believe their organization's culture is critical to business success.

60% Said culture is more important than company's strategy or operating model.

96% Said some form of culture change is needed within their organization.

51% Believe their organization is in need of a major culture overhaul.

45% Do not think their culture is being effectively managed.

Leaders must learn how to tap company culture as an enabler of speed, so this essential asset can become fuel for profitable growth in a change-driven era.

"Culture and Change Management Survey", conducted by Booz & Company (now PwC), Nov 2013.

Figure 1.2 **Results of the culture and change management survey conducted by Booz & Company.**

performance feedback and aptness of *rewards*; the *clarity* people have about mission and values; and finally the level of *commitment* to a common purpose.

Considering the decreasing tenures of the CEOs at any one organization, the irony, however, is that their focus tends to be on delivering short-term tangible benefits with heavy reliance on change management, continuous process improvement methodologies, and HR initiatives, instead of building a long-term organizational culture, which is typically understood as warm and fuzzy. Time and again, it has been proven that investing in culture assessment and alignment

- pays rich dividends over the entire life of your strategy plan
- assists you to align your strategy and operations with the desired culture
- helps you in prioritizing projects that will deliver best value to customers/patients and their families
- increases staff morale
- generates remarkable growth
- improves bottom-line results
- optimizes use of your organization's resources

Choice of Models in the Realm of Culture

While several models and their associated instruments are available to measure culture, the following models are often discussed in the literature:

- Competing Values Framework
- Denison culture model
- Hofsede culture model
- Barrett model
- Human synergistics circumplex model
- Deal and Kennedy's culture model
- Trompenaars and Hampden-Turner's culture dimensions model

An Approach to Organizational Culture Assessment

I am sharing below a unique approach to culture assessment and alignment that I designed and implemented at several organizations across different industries. This approach is based on the Competing Values Framework and is explained using five stages to manage the implementation (Figure 1.3):

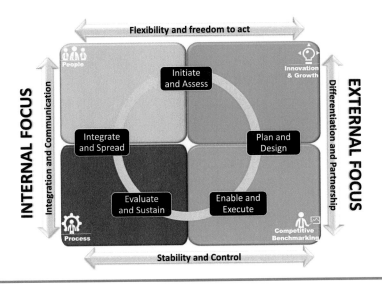

Figure 1.3 **An approach to culture assessment.**

- A. Initiate and assess
- B. Plan and design
- C. Enable and execute
- D. Evaluate and sustain
- E. Integrate and spread

I will detail the first three stages, which pertain to assessing organization culture, in this chapter, and the last two stages will be addressed in Chapter 5, where I describe how to align and integrate culture with organizational strategy. The sets of activities undertaken in each stage, as detailed below, are very engaging and structured but at the same time flexible and agile. They can be adapted to the needs of the stakeholders to deliver the expected outcome.

A. Initiate and assess
1. Understand, review, and confirm the mandate.
2. Establish a steering committee for the overall initiative.
3. Identify stakeholders.
4. Conduct one-on-one meetings and structured conversations with all key stakeholders.
5. Draft a charter that clearly defines expectations, goals, deliverables, in-scope, out-scope, stakeholders, relevant metrics, and timeframe.
6. Finalize a small planning group that includes a single point of contact (POC) for coordinating all logistics, scheduling meetings and

workshops, and assisting in data requests and retrievals for the initiative.

 7. Review the current strategic plan, vision, and values of the organization.
 8. Review and analyze operational reports of departments.
 9. Understand the strengths and weaknesses of the organization.
 10. Review the current structure of the organization.

B. Plan and design

 1. Ascertain the number of stakeholders and the most meaningful configuration in which to group them for conducting the culture assessment.
 2. Develop a comprehensive communications plan along with the organization's communication team that outlines objectives, tactics, target audiences, and a multiplatform strategy for engagement.
 3. Finalize dates and logistics for conducting workshops.
 4. Plan for circulating educational and reference material for self-reading to groups prior to participating in the workshops.
 5. Prepare the education material for teaching stakeholders about
    a. The initiative and approach,
    b. The different types and attributes of change,
    c. The definition of the organization's culture and its types and attributes,
    d. The relationship between culture and strategy,
    e. The role of leadership in an organization's culture, and
    f. The application and benefits of the Competing Values Framework.
 6. Plan and design the approach for administering the OCAI in a live setting during the workshops.
 7. Plan for sharing the results with all stakeholders to understand the current state of perspectives of different groups and individuals.

C. Enable and execute

 1. Conduct education sessions for all identified stakeholders.
 2. Provide operational definitions for all six dimensions of the OCAI.
 3. Administer the OCAI in a live workshop setting to understand the current state (Table 1.1).
    a. Quantitative assessment:
       i. Measure the current state of the organizational culture.
       ii. Analyze the results of the current state, demonstrate similarities and differences in different groups, and share them with all stakeholder groups.

Table 1.1 Organization Culture Assessment Instrument Adapted from Cameron/Quinn

Organizational Culture Assessment Instrument			
Name: _____		Date: _____	
Title & Department: _____		Organization: _____	
1. Dominant characteristics		**Now**	**Preferred**
A	The organization is a very personal place. It is like an extended family. People seem to share a lot of themselves.		
B	The organization is a very dynamic entrepreneurial place, continually exploring the potential for growth. People are willing to take calculated risks.		
C	The organization is very results oriented. Emphasis is on getting the job done. People are very competitive and achievement oriented.		
D	The organization is a very controlled and structured place. Formal procedures, measurements, and monitoring systems generally govern what people do.		
	Total	**100**	**100**
2. Organizational leadership		**Now**	**Preferred**
A	The leadership in the organization is generally considered to exemplify mentoring, facilitating, or nurturing.		
B	The leadership in the organization is generally considered to exemplify venturing into new opportunities, creative problem solving, or risk taking.		
C	The leadership in the organization is generally considered to exemplify a target-driven, aggressive, results-oriented focus.		

(Continued)

Table 1.1 (*Continued*)   Organization Culture Assessment Instrument Adapted from Cameron/Quinn

Organizational Culture Assessment Instrument			
Name: _____		Date: _____	
Title & Department: _____		Organization: _____	
D	The leadership in the organization is generally considered to exemplify coordinating and organizing activities for smooth, cost-efficient business management.		
	Total	100	100
3. Management of employees		**Now**	**Preferred**
A	The management style in the organization is characterized by teamwork, consensus, and participation.		
B	The management style in the organization is characterized by individual risk taking, creative problem solving, freedom, and uniqueness.		
C	The management style in the organization is characterized by hard-driving competitiveness, high demands, and achievement.		
D	The management style in the organization is characterized by conformity, predictability, and stability in relationships.		
	Total	100	100
4. Organizational glue		**Now**	**Preferred**
A	The glue that holds the organization together is loyalty and mutual trust. Commitment to this organization runs high.		
B	The glue that holds the organization together is commitment to innovation and continuous improvement. There is an emphasis on being on the cutting edge.		

(Continued)

Table 1.1 (*Continued*) **Organization Culture Assessment Instrument Adapted from Cameron/Quinn**

Organizational Culture Assessment Instrument			
Name: _____		Date: _____	
Title & Department: _____		Organization: _____	
C	The glue that holds the organization together is the emphasis on achievement and goal accomplishment. Aggressiveness and winning are common themes.		
D	The glue that holds the organization together is formal policies and operating structures. Maintaining a smooth-running organization is important.		
	Total	100	100
5. Strategic emphases		**Now**	**Preferred**
A	The organization emphasizes human development. High trust, openness, and participation persist.		
B	The organization emphasizes acquiring new resources and creating new challenges. Trying new things and prospecting for future growth opportunities are valued.		
C	The organization emphasizes competitive actions, benchmarking, and achievement. Hitting stretch targets and winning in the marketplace are dominant.		
D	The organization emphasizes continuity and stability. Efficiency, control, and smooth operations are important.		
	Total	100	100
6. Criteria of success		**Now**	**Preferred**
A	The organization defines success on the basis of the development of human resources, teamwork, employee commitment, and concern for people.		

(Continued)

Table 1.1 (*Continued*) **Organization Culture Assessment Instrument Adapted from Cameron/Quinn**

Organizational Culture Assessment Instrument			
Name: _____		**Date:** _____	
Title & Department: _____		**Organization:** _____	
B	The organization defines success on the basis of developing a culture of creative problem solving. It is a leader in demonstrating best practice and innovative service offerings.		
C	The organization defines success on the basis of winning in the marketplace and outpacing the competition. Competitive market leadership is key.		
D	The organization defines success on the basis of efficiency. Dependable delivery, smooth scheduling, and low operational costs are critical.		
	Total	**100**	**100**

Source: Cameron/Quinn, Diagnosing and Changing Organizational Culture, ©2000.

    b. Qualitative assessment:
       i. Facilitate open discussion with teams to share their thought processes on the reasons for those differences and similarities.
      ii. Facilitate structured discussions for teams to diverge and then converge on what the desired culture of the organization should be in the future state.
  4. Administer the OCAI in a live workshop setting to understand the desired future state.
    a. Quantitative assessment:
       i. Measure the future state of the organizational culture.
      ii. Analyze the results of the future state and demonstrate the differences between the current and future states.
    b. Qualitative assessment:
       i. Facilitate open discussion with teams to share their thought processes on how to bridge the gap between the current state and the desired future state.

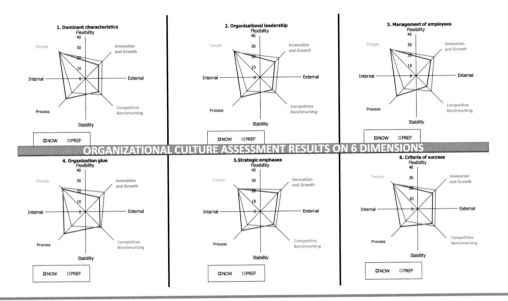

Figure 1.4   **Sample quantitative assessment of current and desired future state of organizational culture on six dimensions.**

ii. Facilitate structured discussions for teams to diverge and then converge on a shared desired future state of the organization's culture.

5. Agree upon the cultural quadrants of the Competing Values Framework that the organization needs to focus on to build congruency and leverage its strengths (Figure 1.4).

6. Facilitate a workshop to develop an action plan and align the current projects/initiatives with the desired culture.

7. Share best-practice management system frameworks and the infrastructure changes required to build a sustainable desired future organizational culture with senior management.

Sensei Gyaan: *Hire a Lean sensei to guide you through the excellence journey. It will be the most wise investment decision that you as a leader will make in your organization. An experienced sensei will keep the organization focused and help the organization navigate its unique cycle in the change curve.*

Chapter 2

Select the Change Approach That Is Right for Your Organization

I can't change the direction of the wind, but I can adjust my sails to always reach my destination.

—Jimmy Dean

The assessment informs the nature and size of the opportunities for improvement. Understanding the characteristics of these opportunities is critical in identifying and selecting the type of change required that will best meet the needs of your organization. Most organizations fail to realize that selecting the correct type of change approach is one of the most crucial steps in their excellence journey. An incorrect selection of the change type at this stage leads to failed efforts or disappointing results. In other words, the wrong approach equals wrong results. To help choose the right approach, let's now learn about the different types of change and their characteristics.

All kinds of change can be broadly categorized under three types (Figure 2.1).

Incremental Change: As the name suggests, the change is incremental in nature. It is a small step-by-step improvement on previous performance over time. Typically, this problem is confined within a department or function. It is known and experienced by the frontline during daily operations. In Figure 2.2, F1, F2, and F3 represent functions and the dots represent the

| Incremental Change | Transitional Change | Transformational Change |

Figure 2.1   Types of change.

problem that could be anywhere in that functional area. Oftentimes, possible solutions to the problem are known; they just need to be implemented according to which one best meets the requirements.

An individual or a small working group comes together and solves the problem within a day or at most within four weeks. The motivation for undertaking an incremental change is to gain efficiency. The scientific approach to problem solving—Plan Do Study Adjust (PDSA); the seven quality tools (flow chart, histogram, cause-and-effect diagram, check sheet, scatter diagram, control chart, and Pareto chart), and the basic Lean Thinking tool kit are mostly sufficient to address the problems in this category.

Transitional Change: If the problem is more complex than an incremental change could solve, it requires more effort, more data analysis, a higher degree of problem solving tools and structure, and more time and resources to bridge the gap between the current and desired future state. The solution to the problem may or may not be known, but steps toward the new state can be defined, managed, implemented, and controlled within a scheduled timeframe. The problem could occur in a functional area or it could be organization-wide. In Figure 2.3, vertical lines F1, F2, and F3 represent a scope confined to functional areas; the horizontal lines P/S 1, P/S 2, and P/S 3 represent multiple touchpoints

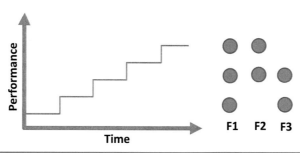

Figure 2.2   Incremental change.

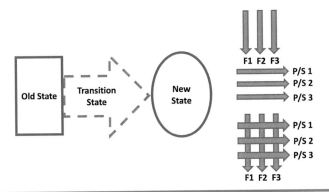

Figure 2.3   **Transitional change.**

of different functions that are involved in delivering the product/service; and the meshed grid represents a combination of both.

The motivation for undertaking transitional change is not only to gain efficiency but also effectiveness. In a transitional change, structured project management framework and tools from process improvement methodologies such as Lean, Six Sigma, Process Reengineering, Agile, etc. are leveraged, in addition to the tools used for incremental change. The duration of the project can vary from multiple months to multiple years. It is, however, recommended that larger and longer projects be broken down into phases and deliverables, with each phase restricted to be accomplished in not more than twelve months.

Transformational Change: This type of change is more strategic in nature. The motivation for change is beyond gaining efficiency and effectiveness. It is undertaken only when at least one of the following scenarios are true:

1. The question is of survival and time is of the essence when
   a. There is an external threat of competition,
   b. An organization's product or services have become or are likely to become obsolete, or
   c. An organization is or anticipated to be in fiscal deficit.
2. The existing organizational culture cannot produce the new results that the shareholders/stakeholders need to achieve, which triggers the need for the organizational culture to change. Some of the other triggers that may call for a culture change are installation of a new CEO, a merger, and a spin-off.

Transformational change is not for everyone. If your organization does not fall into any of the scenarios mentioned above, you do not require a transformational change—period.

In an HBR article, Ron Ashkenas, coauthor of *The GE Work-Out* and *The Boundaryless Organization*, differentiates between change management and transformational change. He explains that *change management* means implementing finite initiatives, which may or may not cut across the organization. The focus is on executing a well-defined shift in the way things work. During a transformational change, you implement a portfolio of initiatives, which can be independent or intersecting with the goal not just to execute a defined change but to reinvent the organization based on a vision for the future.

In a transformational change journey, the future is unknown when you begin and is determined through trial and error, discovering and learning, as new information is gathered. The tools, frameworks, and methodologies used for incremental change and transitional change are helpful but not sufficient. It requires a new management system model that impacts change at a system level and fundamentally changes the way the business is currently run (Figure 2.4). When the change process is complete, the prior organization is no longer recognizable.

Transformation results in new forms of being that bear little resemblance to what existed before—a true paradigm shift. Paradigm shifts are movements from one primary world view and way of operating to a radically different one. Chris McGoff, author of *The Primes*, says, "A butterfly is a transformation, not a better caterpillar." In incremental and transitional change, the desire to improve the past directs what we do. The past sets boundaries and constrains possibilities. In a transformational change, the future directs your actions and only the limits of imagination and courage constrain possibilities.

Transformational change requires a high degree of mental and emotional strength as it can be chaotic and emotionally draining at times,

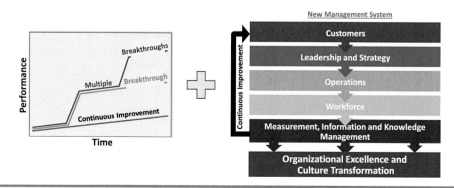

Figure 2.4   **Transformational change.**

when individuals feel lost in their ability to estimate the duration of the ongoing constant change. During this phase, many people, including some leaders, expect to see a clear step-by-step roadmap for change laid out, and change facilitators have no choice but to pacify teams by providing Gantt charts and schedules from project management. Unfortunately, transformational change cannot be managed with a linear and time-bound plan. The period of change in the mindset and behavior of a critical mass of the organization cannot be predetermined. What can be managed though are the parts of the transformation that require elements of incremental and transitional change.

Since most people are not comfortable being in the unknown zone for very long, it is the leadership's responsibility to keep the organization focused, engaged, and on the transformational path. It is not uncommon to see leaders themselves losing steam midway. In that situation, the CEO assumes responsibility for reenergizing people across the organization.

When an organization is in survival mode, all hands are on deck. You need multiple breakthroughs, fast. You do not have the time to rely purely on incremental improvements for keeping the lights on. You need to implement incremental improvements, transitional improvements, and a new management system model—all simultaneously. Unlike in other change types, the CEO creates the vision and owns the implementation of the high-level plan by enabling systems and structures. Prompt decision making with clearly defined non-negotiables takes precedence over consensus building. There is a heavy focus on executing, building trust, and respecting one another while experiencing challenges during implementation. Continued fast-paced experimentation and corrective actions are undertaken, i.e., a PDSA on steroids replaces a traditional PDSA. Intensive support is provided to solicit ongoing feedback and address stress and emotions that run high due to unpredictability during the transformation period.

Ford, General Electric, and Apple, to name a few, are all examples of organizations that have gone through turbulent times but have bounced back, bigger and stronger. Not to discount the importance of engaging the frontline, the middle management, and other senior executives who played key roles during the transformational journey in these organizations, it was the CEOs who followed through with their vision to make it a reality.

On the other hand, when an organization is not in survival mode and the intent is either to improve the business or to build a distinct culture over time by selecting from the CVF mix of four culture types, a great approach is to conduct improvements using traditional PDSA. Teams make incremental changes in their respective processes over time, study and learn from them, and make adjustments to their process to make them better. The organization has the time to educate its staff in the continuous improvement methodology, build consensus, and engage people at all levels across the organization to collaboratively build the new organization—slowly and steadily, one brick at a time. In this case, the organization becomes better organically and may potentially transform over time.

According to Scherrer-Rathje et al., for an organization to be successful at implementing Lean and transforming, it needs to take a top-down approach led by senior management and based on change within the whole organization's culture, system, and thinking. Management is responsible for strategic direction (top down) and improvement work is managed by employees (bottom up). The bottom-up approach, by itself, is not sustainable. When applied it usually forms small isolated islands of Lean work, which has a risk of people reverting back to previous practices. The system therefore must be implemented using a top-down approach, but built from the bottom up, and it must have the support of the entire organization.

As mentioned earlier, it is unfortunate that specific process improvement tools and methodologies that are best suited for incremental and transitional change are being promoted as silver bullets for a transformational change. The tools for incremental change and transitional change are powerful and work when the organization is stable. These tools, without being supplemented by elements of the management system, can neither change employee behavior to affect organizational culture nor turn the organization around when it is struggling.

In their book, *Bringing Leadership to Life in Health*, Graham Dickson and Bill Tholl write, "We need to move from incremental change to purposeful reform—the difference being that change is a single act, while reform is a process." In a turbulent environment when nothing is predictable, courageous leadership is needed.

Detailed Comparison of Critical Characteristics for the Three Types of Change

Based on my practical experience from more than two decades in the area of organizational excellence, supported by best-practice academic literature and leveraged shared experiences of several leaders and consultants, I have provided in Table 2.1 a detailed comparison of the three types of change.

Summing-up: Incremental change is seen as a slow process, which modifies the landscape only slightly. If implementation of small changes is done over a long period of time, it leads to a more efficient organization over time. Transition is seen as a fluent change toward a new future, which is an improved version of the existing organization, but transformation is seen as a change toward a future that is fundamentally different from the existing organization. The transformational change offers the best perspective in dealing with uncertain, unexpected, and unprecedented futures (Figure 2.5).

Sensei Gyaan: *As a leader, understand the characteristics, expected deliverables, and limitations of each change type before selecting the change approach that is right for your organization. This will allow you to set realistic expectations from the change journey and help you and your team avoid unnecessary frustrations along the way. Practitioners and leaders can use Table 2.2 as a rule of thumb for selecting the type of change in their organization. Also, I encourage leaders to ask these questions:*

1. *What is my motivation for change? Am I concerned about efficiency, effectiveness, or behavior change?*
2. *Do I have a culture that will get me the new results I want to achieve?*

Table 2.1 Comparison of Critical Characteristics for Three Types of Change

Parameter	Incremental Change	Transitional Change	Transformational Change
Definition	• Tweaking of the system or process. A new state is prescribed as an enhancement of the old state. • Change occurs over a period of time in incremental stages.	• Implementation of a known new state. • Management of the interim transition state over a controlled period of time. • Change is at the subsystem level. Focus is internal and on integration. May or may not cut across the organization.	• Emergence of a radically different new state, unknown until it takes shape. • The new state requires a fundamental shift in mindset, behavior, and/or culture. • Change is at the system level. Focus is external and on differentiation. More strategic in nature. Impacts entire organization.
Conditions	• You can determine your destination before you begin. • You implement a well-scoped initiative with a defined process and outcome metrics.	• You can determine your destination before you begin • You implement a well-scoped initiative with a defined process and outcome metrics.	• The future is unknown when you begin and is determined through trial and error, discovering and learning, as new information is gathered. • You implement a portfolio of initiatives, which can be independent or intersecting with the goal of not just executing a defined change but reinventing the organization based on a vision for the future. • You cannot manage this project with a linear and time-bound plan, since the period of change in mindset and behavior of a critical mass of the organization cannot be predetermined.

(Continued)

Table 2.1 (Continued) Comparison of Critical Characteristics for Three Types of Change

Parameter	Incremental Change	Transitional Change	Transformational Change
Motivation for Change	Efficiency	Effectiveness	• Survival • Environment change • World change • Culture change • Breakthrough
Typical Words Associated	• Problem solving • Repair • Evaluate • Correct • Adjust • Consistent • Uniformity • Increase • Reduce • Root-cause analysis • Train • Coordinate • Structure • Control	• Move forward • Relocate • Transfer • Reposition • Realign • Participate • Collaborate • Re-engineer • Agile • Adaptable • Flexible • Mentor • Consensus • Work breakdown structure	• Create • Uncover • Construct • Generate • Initiate • Discover • Entrepreneurial • Liberate • Invent/innovate • Explore • Let go of • New possibilities • Visioning • Risk taking
Creator of Sense of Urgency	Any team member, manager, or director	Manager, director, or vice president	Board or CEO

(Continued)

Table 2.1 (*Continued*) Comparison of Critical Characteristics for Three Types of Change

Parameter	Incremental Change	Transitional Change	Transformational Change
Deployment approach and stakeholder engagement	• Vice president/director acts as sponsor[a] and approves project business case, charter, funding, and necessary resource requirements. If no special funding or additional resources are required, the director may act as a sponsor, in which case the manager acts as a champion. • The champion develops project charter and assigns the project lead and team members.	• Vice president acts as sponsor and approves project business case, charter, funding, and necessary resource requirements. • Director acts as champion of the project, develops project charter, and assigns the project lead and team members. • Project lead develops and implements a detailed project plan with support from team members and a facilitator, who is trained in the specified management methodology.	• CEO creates the vision and owns the implementation of the high-level plan by enabling systems and structures with representation from all key areas of the organization. • Leaders and influencers are engaged in assimilating the vision to the frontline of the organization. • Core team develops a roadmap and builds a foundation based on best practice and inputs from subject matter experts and other stakeholders. There is a heavy focus on executing, building trust, and respecting one another while experiencing challenges during implementation.

(Continued)

Table 2.1 (*Continued*) Comparison of Critical Characteristics for Three Types of Change

Parameter	Incremental Change	Transitional Change	Transformational Change
	• Project lead along with team members develops the current state and establishes the new future state process. Project lead may request for facilitator support, if needed. • Project lead ensures stakeholder engagement throughout the project. Decisions are based on consensus. • Team test pilots the new process/method and continues to perform PDSA until the new process is repeatable and reliable. • Formal evaluation of the process and sustainability plan established. Project documents are completed and the project is closed by the sponsor.	• Project lead and facilitator ensure stakeholder engagement throughout the transition period. Decisions are based on consensus. • Team test pilots the solution and continues to perform PDSA until defects are eliminated and the new state delivers the desired performance. • Formal evaluation of the process and sustainability plan established. Project documentation completed and project closed by sponsor. • Team celebrates after accomplishing desired milestone(s).	• Intensive support provided to solicit ongoing feedback and to address stress and emotions that run high, due to unpredictability, during the transformation period. Prompt decision making with clearly defined non-negotiables takes precedence over consensus building. • Continued fast-paced experimentation and discovery celebrated along the transformational journey. PDSA on steroids replaces traditional PDSA. No formal evaluation process established until later. Focus is on reinforcing vision and encouraging behavior change to affect culture. • Approach modified/changed until the new state emerges and/or expected threshold is surpassed. Further change can be managed using an incremental or transitional approach.

(*Continued*)

Table 2.1 (*Continued*) Comparison of Critical Characteristics for Three Types of Change

Parameter	Incremental Change	Transitional Change	Transformational Change
	• For "just do it", no charter is required. team member initiate, lead, implement and sustain the new process. • Team celebrates after accomplishing desired objective.		• Teams have fun and celebration all along the journey.
Role of a Leader	Support and mentor	Support and guide with compassionate assertiveness	• Lead and direct with compassionate assertiveness. • Leaders demonstrate courage and commitment to new thinking, learning, and actions as they tread through totally uncharted territory.
Impact on employees	Low to medium	Medium to high	High to very high
Need for and frequency of communication	• Medium • Address logical need	• High to very high • Address logical need	• Exponentially high • Address emotional need
Risk identified for	Implementing change	Implementing change	Not implementing change
Environment	Mostly stable	Relatively stable	Least stable
Healthcare parlance	Routine	Urgent, e.g., worsening vital signs post-operative	Stat, e.g., absence of vital signs in emergency

[a] In some parts of the world, the director designation is higher than the vice president, in which case the sponsor is the director.

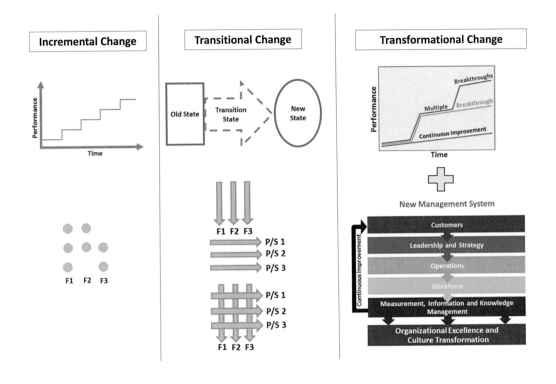

Figure 2.5 Pictorial comparison of the three types of change.

Table 2.2 Rule of Thumb to Select the Type of Change

Current Situation		Staff Readiness to Make Change		
		Resistant	Indifferent	Ready
Low Confidence that change will lead to improvement	Cost of Failure Large	Incremental Change	Incremental Change	Incremental or Transitional Change
	Cost of Failure Small	Incremental Change	Incremental or Transitional Change	Incremental or Transitional Change
High Confidence that change will lead to improvement	Cost of Failure Large	Incremental Change	Incremental or Transitional Change	Incremental or Transitional or Transformational Change
	Cost of Failure Small	Incremental or Transitional Change	Incremental or Transitional or Transformational Change	Incremental or Transitional or Transformational Change

Chapter 3

Select the Framework for Change

You can't go back and change the beginning, but you can start where you are and change the ending.

—C.S. Lewis

Why is implementing change successfully so hard to accomplish? James Belasco and Ralph Stayer say, "Change is hard because people overestimate the value of what they have—and underestimate the value of what they may gain by giving that up." In their book, *Switch: How to Change Things When Change is Hard*, Dan and Chip Heath write, "People have two separate 'systems' in their brains—a rational system and an emotional system. The rational system is a thoughtful, logical planner. The emotional system is, well, emotional—and impulsive and instinctual. When these two systems are in alignment, change can come quickly and easily. When they're not, change can be grueling." Let's first understand the different levels of resistance to change:

Level 1: Based on Information
  – Lack of information
  – Disagreement with the idea itself
  – Lack of exposure
  – Confusion

Level 2: Physiological and Emotional Reactions
  – Loss of power or control
  – Loss of status

- Loss of face or respect
- Feelings of incompetence
- Feelings of isolation and abandonment
- Sense that you can't take on anything else (too much change)
- Fatigue due to continued change over a period of time

Level 3: Bigger than the Current Change
- Personal history of mistrust
- Cultural, ethnic, racial, gender differences
- Significant disagreement over values
- Transference—the person being resisted represents someone else to you or you are reacting to a previous situation

The critical part of the challenge of change is unfreezing what is and refreezing at a new, different, and higher level of performance. An equation commonly used to overcome resistance to change is reflected in Figure 3.1.

While there are several management frameworks and models available in the literature for leading organizational change, those most commonly referred to are

- Lewin's Freeze Phases
- McKinsey's 7S model
- Kotter's change model
- Bridge's transition model
- Change Acceleration Process model
- Adaptive change
- Prosci's ADKAR

No model is superior to any other, as all of these models have been proven to work. It is really a matter of choice and the comfort level of communicating the model within the organization by the change

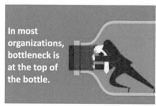

D x V x F > R*
- D = Dissatisfaction, or discontent with the status quo
- V = Vision of the Future
- F = First Steps (laid out...)
- R = Resistance to change

*Only if D, V and F are > 0, we can overcome R

In most organizations, bottleneck is at the top of the bottle.

Figure 3.1   **An equation to overcome resistance to change.**

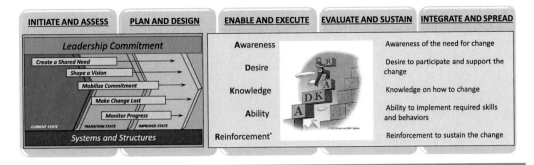

Figure 3.2 Change framework implemented during the transformational journey at Hospital Heal.

practitioner. At an organizational level, I find the Change Acceleration Process (CAP) model to be one of the more robust models for establishing systems and structures and creating a solid foundation, while at an individual change level, I have found Prosci's ADKAR to be more pragmatic (Figure 3.2).

The CAP model was created and practiced successfully under the leadership of Jack Welch, CEO of General Electric in the late 1990s. Even after nearly two decades of its existence, the CAP model (Figure 3.3) is respected for its credibility and is practiced by forward-thinking organizations that believe in investing time to build a strong foundation for change.

Leadership Commitment and Systems and Structures in the CAP model are prerequisites for any change effort and support the

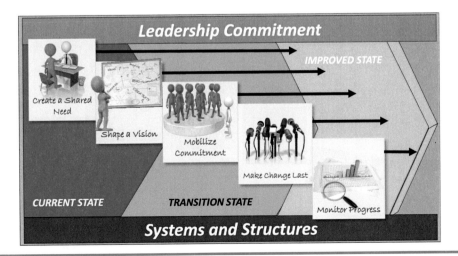

Figure 3.3 Change Acceleration Process (CAP) model.

Table 3.1 Twenty-Six Foundational Elements Represented Under the CAP Model Framework

Cap Model Category	#	Foundational Element	#
Create a shared need	1.1	Understand the need for change	1
	1.2	Select the change approach that is right for your organization	2
	1.3	Select the framework for change	3
	1.4	Integrate the excellence journey with the organization's strategy	4
Shape a vision	2.1	Integrate organizational culture with strategy	5
	2.2	Design a business excellence model to implement the excellence journey	6
Mobilize commitment	3.1	Define roles and responsibilities of change facilitators	7
	3.2	Develop recruitment criteria and select the change facilitators	8
	3.3	Organize visits to best-practice organizations for leaders to "Go See Learn"	9
Make change last	4.1	Develop the organization report card	10
	4.2	Develop a visual strategy room	11
	4.3	Develop the process to cascade the organization strategy to the frontline	12
	4.4	Develop project prioritization and selection criteria	13
	4.5	Prioritize and select the critical few improvement initiatives across the organization	14
	4.6	Define roles and responsibilities of the project teams	15
	4.7	Define the guiding principles and management system elements to sustain the excellence journey	16
	4.8	Develop a communication plan with a high degree of visual management to support branding	17
	4.9	Develop processes to celebrate experiments and to recognize individuals and teams	18

(Continued)

Table 3.1 (*Continued*) Twenty-Six Foundational Elements Represented Under the CAP Model Framework

Cap Model Category	#	Foundational Element	#
	4.10	Develop content for standard work on management system elements and other education material to support the excellence journey	19
	4.11	Build the problem-solving muscle of the organization	20
	4.12	Build a knowledge management system	21
Monitor progress	5.1	Define the role of the performance management team to support the excellence journey	22
	5.2	Develop a standard toll gate process to evaluate the progress of improvement projects	23
	5.3	Develop a five-year roadmap and evaluation criteria for the excellence journey	24
	5.4	Develop evaluation criteria for selecting the test pilot area for implementation	25
	5.5	Develop individual performance measures for leaders to build accountability	26

remaining five categories throughout the course of the excellence journey:

1. Create a shared need
2. Shape a vision
3. Mobilize commitment
4. Make change last
5. Monitor progress

Readers are encouraged to further explore the CAP model and its application, which is beyond the scope of this book.

I have used the CAP model as an overarching framework for change and embedded concepts from different business excellence frameworks and methodologies such as Malcolm Baldrige, Shingo, Balanced Scorecard, Lean, Six Sigma, business process management, patient and family-centered care, Kotter's change model, Prosci's ADKAR, and the Competing Values Framework to design various models, guiding principles, management systems, and foundational elements that you will learn about in the subsequent sections of this book.

Based on my past experience in establishing an infrastructure for transformational change at several organizations, I have put together 26 elements that crystalize the foundation for change and catapults the results of implementation (Table 3.1). These 26 foundational elements have been further elaborated and illustrated through visuals, where applicable, to increase your learning experience, and they correspond to the 26 chapters of this book. A word of caution: These are not IKEA instructions on how to handle change in an organization.

The criticality of the organization's need, however, defines the pace of implementation, which in turn outlines the resource commitment in regard to people and budget for establishing the infrastructure for change.

Sensei Gyaan: *Identify and leverage your change accelerators and change influencers to manage your change detractors.*

SHAPE A VISION

B

Chapter 4

Integrate the Excellence Journey with the Organization's Strategy

If you don't know where you are going, any road will take you there.

—Chinese proverb

Once the organization has committed to embark on the path to excellence, engage teams to develop a name, vision, and guiding principles for the excellence journey.

Often underestimated, a name is one of the key contributors to the success of the excellence journey in an organization. In Chapter 1, we discussed the importance of understanding the need for change, and in Chapter 2 we qualified the magnitude of the change required. A purposeful name inspires people to take action, since it translates the organization's internal need to an external benefit that impacts the customer, patient, or society. It helps people to recognize how their work contributes to the objective of the excellence journey. Take the example of Hospital Heal, which titled its excellence journey "More Time to Care," with this objective: "To develop an organization that empowers people at all levels to optimize their work processes, and partners with patients and their families to improve the patient experience."

On the other hand, if an excellence journey shares the same name as the performance improvement methodology itself, it may not be inspiring enough and could have negative connotations in people's minds. Lean,

Six Sigma, and Agile, among other methodologies, have been associated with making people do more with less or a way to reduce head counts from gaining efficiencies. I have heard sarcastic associations of Lean with "Less Employees Are Needed."

Another important aspect to recognize in the organization is whether the excellence journey is treated as a program, initiative, or an important project in your organization. If it is any of the above, you have made a false start. The leadership commitment can only be acknowledged if the excellence journey has a clearly articulated vision, with guiding principles, and if it is one of the strategic objectives/priorities of the organization's strategic plan. In all other cases, it is lip service. The commitment has to be demonstrated by the CEO for getting the board/trustees to endorse the journey as one of the key strategic drivers to organizational excellence. The guiding principles hold senior leaders accountable to make ethical decisions, especially during the times of adversity, dilemma, and conflict (Table 4.1).

A strategy map is a powerful tool of the Balanced Scorecard framework that visually communicates the cause-and-effect relationships between the strategic objectives and strategic directions for getting buy-in from the board and senior management. Figures 4.1 and 4.2 are examples of how Hospital Heal used the tools of the Balanced Scorecard framework in their communications strategy to demonstrate organizational commitment to their excellence journey, More Time to Care.

Table 4.1 More Time to Care Vision and Guiding Principles Developed at Hospital Heal

Objective of More Time to Care	• To develop an organization that empowers people at all levels to optimize their work processes and partners with patients and families to improve patient experience
Vision	• Guided by our patient and led by our people & partners, we will travel together on our journey towards excellence
Guiding Principles	• All processes will be examined through the patient lens • All projects will be prioritized and aligned to organization's strategic direction • We are going to communicate effectively throughout the journey • All members of team are involved in problem solving • Every improvement idea will be considered • We will encourage and recognize contributions • We will have the courage to experiment with new ideas and celebrate our learnings • We will offer retraining opportunities to people displaced through improvement activities • We will be consistent and just in our approach • We have an expectation of high performance and participation in excellence journey by our people • We will establish mechanisms to sustain improvements • We will be generous and inclusive with our partners • We will deploy Creativity before Capital investment

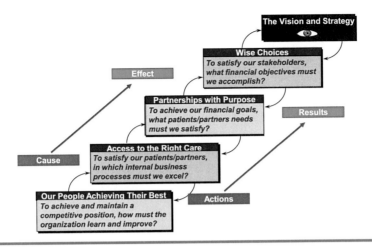

Figure 4.1 Hospital Heal's strategic directions reflected as perspectives of the Balanced Scorecard framework.

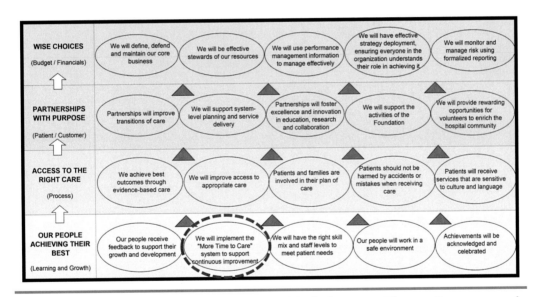

Figure 4.2 The strategy map of Hospital Heal includes More Time to Care as one of their key strategic objectives.

Sensei Gyaan*: (i) Senior leaders—Don't create any guiding principle for the excellence journey that you cannot live up to. (ii) Practitioners—Don't bother to initiate the excellence journey in your organization if it is not a priority of the CEO. Even one designation below won't cut it.*

Chapter 5

Integrate Organizational Culture with Strategy

Who needs goals, when you can develop new good habits. Don't focus on achieving any goals. Instead, aim to develop the behavior that creates long-lasting habits and wields the results you want as a byproduct.

—Jeff Boss

While a CEO's commitment is critical in an organization's transformation journey, it is also important that people are culturally ready to support the implementation of the strategy. In Chapter 1, I shared an approach for undertaking an organizational culture assessment to understand the current state and to develop a shared vision by engaging leaders at all levels to agree on the desired future state. In this chapter, we will learn about a model that helps to integrate organizational culture with strategy. We will also uncover the last two stages of the culture assessment and alignment that we initiated in Chapter 1.

Organizational culture can be defined as a set of values, beliefs, and assumptions, demonstrated as behavior by individuals in a particular environment. If you dissect this definition a little bit, you will realize that there are two critical components, behavior and environment, both of which are essential ingredients for a culture change. The values, beliefs, and assumptions held by individuals are unseen constituents but have a strong influence on the people in the organization and dictate how they act, interact with others, and perform their jobs. At the same time, an organization's environment has to be conducive to allow the desired behaviors to be exhibited.

The culture of the organization is heavily influenced by its leaders. Leadership sets the tone for behaviors expected from the staff in an organization, and individuals and teams change their behaviors to match the expectations of their leaders. Frontline staff and support staff who directly or indirectly interact with patients/customers provide valuable information about the mood of the organization. However, these groups have lower influence on changing the current and desired culture of an organization. Customers/patients and families provide valuable feedback and insight on cost, quality, and delivery expectations of the product/service offered by the organization, which in turn guides leadership in setting the vision. However, to internalize the behavior expectations that influence the culture of the organization is the responsibility of leadership.

Zappos, Southwest Airlines, Warby Parker, Google, the Mayo Clinic, Apple, Procter & Gamble, IBM, Cleveland Clinic, and Kaiser Permanente, to name a few leading organizations, have made cultural identity as a part of their competitive advantage. Their leaders didn't stumble into the culture they desired—they deliberately created it. It is therefore not striking to see how many chief executives see their most important responsibility as being the leader of the company's culture. According to Ginni Rometty, CEO of IBM, "Culture is your company's number one asset." Steve Ballmer, erstwhile CEO of Microsoft, said, "Everything I do is a reinforcement or not of what we want to have happen culturally." In another remark from the C-suite, George C Halvorson, former CEO of Kaiser Permanente, largest nonprofit health plan and hospital system in the United States, serving more than 9 million members and generating about $50 billion in annual revenue, in the HBR article, "Culture to Cultivate," said "Continuous improvement is the only cultural value that could unify an organization as large and diverse as ours."

The CEO is the most visible leader in a company. His or her direct engagement in all facets of the company's culture can make an enormous difference, not just in how people feel about the company, but in how they perform. Howard Schultz, former CEO of Starbucks Corporation, described the CEO's role this way in his book *Onward: How Starbucks Fought for Its Life without Losing Its Soul*: "Like crafting the perfect cup of coffee, creating an engaging, respectful, trusting workplace culture is not the result of any one thing. It's a combination of intent, process, and heart, a trio that must constantly be fine-tuned."

In their article, "Culture and the Chief Executive," Jon Katzenbach and DeAnne Aguirre, leaders at Strategy& list the following four asks from a CEO to spark and foster the cultural realignments they want to see:

- Demonstrate positive urgency by focusing on your company'saspirations—its unfulfilled potential—rather than on any impending crisis.
- Pick a critical few behaviors that exemplify the best of your company and culture, and that you want everyone to adopt. Set an example by visibly adopting a couple of these behaviors yourself.
- Balance your appeals to the company to include both rational and emotional cues.
- Make the change sustainable by maintaining vigilance on the few critical elements that you have established as important.

Long story short, in a transformational journey, culture change starts in the executive suite. Top leaders need to define the culture, communicate it to all organizational levels, act and behave in ways that reflect and reinforce desired outcomes and take responsibility for aligning and integrating culture, strategy, and operations. Leadership development can play a key role in accelerating, reinforcing, and sustaining culture change throughout the organization.

Readers familiar with strategic planning and deployment will appreciate that the four perspectives of the Balanced Scorecard (BSC—a framework for strategic performance management), namely, learning and growth, process, customer, and financial, resonate well with the quadrants of the Competing Values Framework (CVF), namely, people, process, innovation and growth, and competitive benchmarking. The quadrant terminology in CVF is more explicit, though, in compelling organizations to think about innovation and growth, and competitive benchmarking while designing their strategy to enable them to continuously improve upon their performance. To be competitive in the marketplace you have to be customer centered and develop products and services in partnership with customers.

Acknowledging that each organization is a mix of four culture types, namely, people, process, innovation and growth, and competitive benchmarking, and that each strategy is also a mix of the same four components, I have used CVF as the base model and included in it the leadership and structure components of CAP model, that were introduced in Chapter 3, to create a new model that integrates leadership, structure, organizational culture, and strategy (Figure 5.1).

Leaders and practitioners are encouraged to use this model for engaging internal and external stakeholders to develop their organization strategy. The constituents of this model will remind all stakeholders to consider the following aspects while designing their organization strategy:

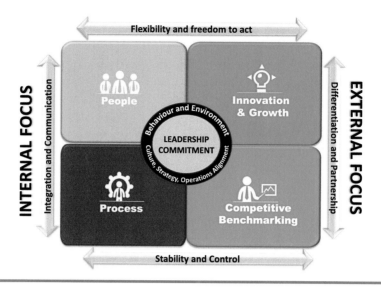

Figure 5.1 Integrated model of organization culture and strategy.

1. People development and accountability
2. Operational effectiveness through process optimization
3. Innovation and creativity
4. New products, services, markets, and geographies to increase revenue
5. Product/service offerings that differentiate them from others
6. Partnerships with customers/patients/communities/suppliers to codesign products/services
7. Creating value through integration
8. Using language that is easy to understand, relate, and communicate
9. Leadership as role model
10. Ensuring alignment among culture, strategy, and operations
11. Setting up the right organizational values
12. Defining the behavior expectations from people
13. Designing systems and structure to provide an environment for people to live values, daily (LOVE—Live Our Values Everyday)
14. Influence of other internal factors
15. Influence of other external factors
16. Designing a strategy that is robust and agile at the same time

Now, with the understanding of the above integrated model, you will be able to appreciate the activities undertaken during the last two stages of the culture assessment and alignment approach shared in Chapter 1 (Figure 5.2).

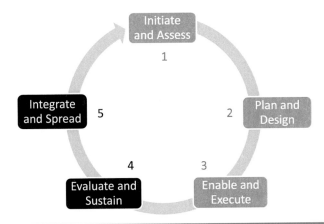

Figure 5.2   **Five stages of a project's life cycle.**

A. Initiate and assess, B. Plan and design, and C. Enable and execute were covered previously. Refer to Chapter 1.

D. Evaluate and sustain

1. Review and revisit the organization's vision, mission, strategic directions, objectives, and priorities.
2. Confirm, amend, or redraft the vision and mission statements and values.
3. Confirm, amend, or redraft the strategic directions and objectives, and establish areas of focus to support the desired future culture.
4. Revisit or redefine roles and responsibilities of different teams and establish agreement how they would support each other to build the new organizational culture.
5. Develop and define the big dot measures (key performance indicators) for the organization strategy based on the desired culture.
6. Define leadership behavior and attributes that will promote the effectiveness of the desired culture quadrant of the Competing Values Framework.
7. Design a maturity scale for measuring organizational culture change.
8. Organization's communication team implements a multiplatform comprehensive strategy for engaging all staff and opens lines of communication that will promote how, when, and what cultural values are important moving forward to reflect the new culture.
9. Develop leaders for identified cultural attributes and establish standard work for these leaders.
10. Create a personal improvement plan and accountability targets with defined timelines to improve leadership competencies.

11. Develop issues resolution and a review process.
12. Evaluate and report team progress toward the desired culture using a maturity scale.
13. Seek steering committee interventions to overcome any structural and environmental barriers to change.
14. Solicit formal and informal feedback from stakeholders during the cultural transformation.

E. Integrate and spread

1. Facilitate establishment of criteria for identification, selection, and prioritization of opportunities, initiatives, and projects to support the new culture (Figure 5.3).
2. Develop an action plan for each group aligned to organization strategy and the desired future culture.
3. Identify quick win opportunities and strategies that can be implemented immediately and will demonstrate visible results for creating positive momentum in the organization.
4. Share and celebrate successes along the culture change journey.
5. Conduct failure mode effects analysis (FMEA) to proactively plan to mitigate any risk and take corrective measures.
6. Cross-pollinate learning between functions and departments.
7. Establish standard work.

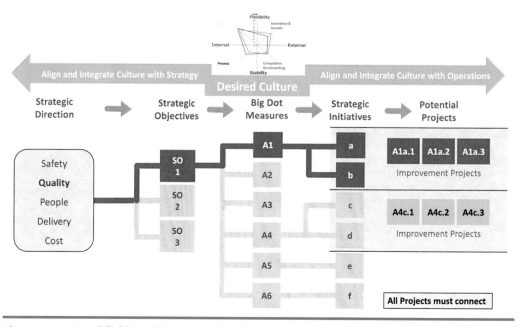

Figure 5.3 **Establishing alignment of culture, strategy, and operations.**

8. Train, coach, and mentor teams to increase spread and maturity of culture change across the organization.
9. Develop and implement a management system framework to align strategy with desired culture and integrate into daily operations.
10. Establish a knowledge management system to document lessons learned at pre-established milestones and continue the culture change journey by updating new targets each year in the charter.

Sensei Gyaan: *As a leader, challenge yourself to first shift your own paradigm from referring to the excellence journey as one of your organization's strategic objectives/priorities to making the excellence journey itself the organization's strategy.*

Chapter 6

Design a Business Excellence Model to Implement the Excellence Journey

If you think you can or you think you can't, you're absolutely right.

—Henry Ford

According to the 2017 PEX Network's, "Global State of Process Excellence" report 38% of respondents said that the current scope of their process deployment was enterprise wide—this is an increase of 2% from 2015 (Figure 6.1). At the same time, the small-scale pilot implementation has also increased from 13% to 14%. It is heartening to know that the percentage of organizations with no process excellence programs have reduced from 10% to 8%. As process reaches a higher position on the corporate agenda, it is anticipated that this number will continue to reduce and in the next few years, the majority of companies will have adopted operational excellence methodologies and tools on a large scale.

Realizing the impact that operational excellence has on an organization, there is a clear movement in leaders considering enterprise-wide models and frameworks for their organizational excellence journey. Some of the most popular business excellence models include

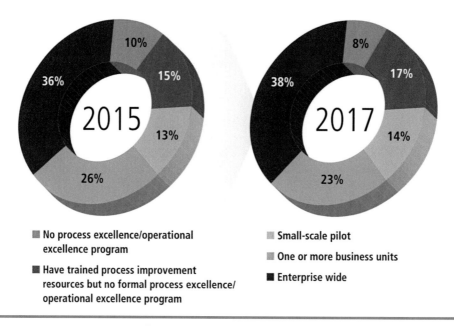

Figure 6.1 2017 PEX Network's Global State of Process Excellence Results.

1. Malcom Baldrige
2. Shingo
3. EFQM (European Foundation for Quality Management, Figure 6.2)

    While some organizations select their deployment approach directly based on any of the above best practice models, others create a customized model to suit their organization culture. In terms of an infrastructural design to support the deployment, organizations have an option either to create a centralized, decentralized, or combination model, depending upon what accountability culture, leaders want to build among individuals and teams in their organization. Remember, an organization's cultural operating system operates by a set of rules that guide employee behavior. For that reason, some of the best practice organizations align operational excellence with human resource function. Joseph Grenny, Cofounder of VitalSmarts, says, "The question is not whether you have a cultural operating system—it's whether yours is one that advances or impedes continuous improvement."

    Figure 6.3 shows a model that was custom developed for implementing More Time to Care at Hospital Heal. This model included key attributes of other best-practice models indicated above. In terms of structure, it included a combination of a centralized and decentralized team that supported the implementation.

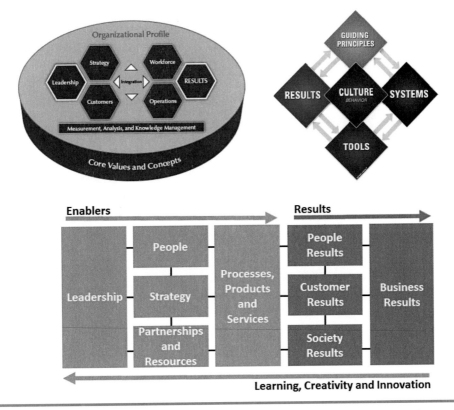

Figure 6.2   Models: Malcom Baldrige (top left), Shingo (top right), EFQM (bottom).

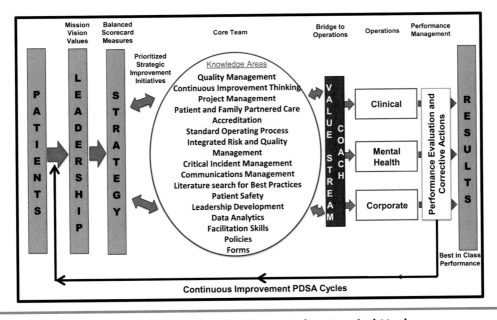

Figure 6.3   Business excellence model implemented at Hospital Heal.

How the Model Works

The patients guide the leadership to develop an organizational strategy that delivers the best measurable patient outcomes. The gaps identified in the process and outcome measures are taken up as strategic initiatives for improvement. A central core team comprises individuals that have expertise in the knowledge areas listed in the model. "Value stream coach," a new position and title created to support the excellence journey, is a full-time dedicated resource taken from frontline operations and seconded for a period of thirty months. First, he or she undergoes training with the core team for an initial period of six months and then subsequently facilitates change in the operational areas of clinical, mental health, and corporate for the remaining period of twenty-four months, thereby serving as a bridge to operations. Upon completion of his or her tenure, the individual assumes a leadership role in the organization and is replaced by a new value stream coach. The performance management team assists in evaluating the performance of projects, initiatives, and organizational change. The feedback is continuously provided to the patients and corrective actions, where required, are taken to address the gaps and deliver best-in-class results.

Resource Deployment to Support the Model

Hospital Heal dedicated six full-time resources as value stream coaches (two each from clinical, mental health, and corporate areas) who worked with the core team members from the departments of Quality & Performance Excellence, Education, and Enterprise Risk Management to deliver projects and to establish standard work across the organization. In addition to the value stream coaches, one full-time "data specialist," part of the performance management department, supported all teams across the organization to define the metrics associated with quality improvement projects and their respective scorecards, establish the formula and baseline, and analyze and trend data. For physicians, a dedicated CQI (continuous quality improvement) coordinator was assigned to support the physician group and integrate their work with not only the hospital operations but also with the components of the organization's excellence journey. A More Time to Care council was established with representatives from all key areas across the organization. The members of the council volunteered to work in small teams and participated in the development of the foundational elements of the excellence journey. The council met once a month to share their progress with other teams and also acted as an excellent communications resource to other employees in the organization.

Sensei Gyaan: *Invest in full-time dedicated resources to facilitate the excellence journey. Note that one full-time resource is better than two operational staff expected to work part time on the journey. Allocate the budget for the resource from the existing operational budget to increase senior leadership commitment.*

MOBILIZE
COMMITMENT

C

Chapter 7

Define the Roles and Responsibilities of the Change Facilitators

A lot of people have gone further than they thought they could because someone else thought they could.

—Zig Ziglar

Depending upon the model and the structure that you design for the excellence journey in your organization, you need to develop job descriptions for all positions (as per the approved budget) that will be directly responsible

Table 7.1 Example of a Template for Mapping Current and Future State Job Responsibilities

CURRENT STATE				FUTURE STATE				ADDITIONAL COMMENTS
JOB TITLE	#	RESPONSIBILITIES	%	JOB TITLE	#	RESPONSIBILITIES	%	
	A				A			
	B				B			
	C				C			
	D				D			
	E				E			
	F				F			
			Total 100%				*Total* 100%	
	A				A			
	B				B			
	C				C			
	D				D			
	E				E			
	F				F			
			Total 100%				*Total* 100%	

for supporting the implementation. Whether you are redefining an existing role or creating a new position, it is good practice to first develop a broad outline of responsibilities for the position before creating a detailed job description. Create a summary in a before and after format for all positions expected to undergo change. A sample ready-reckoner template to create a responsibility change is provided in Table 7.1. Include the current job title, the number of existing positions with the current job title, the category of responsibility, and the percentage of the total available work time that the

Table 7.2 Mapping Current and Future State Job Responsibilities at Hospital Heal

CURRENT STATE					CHANGE in FUTURE STATE	FUTURE STATE					ADDITIONAL COMMENTS
JOB TITLE	#		RESPONSIBILITIES	%		JOB TITLE	#		RESPONSIBILITIES	%	
Patient Safety Officer	2	A	Critical Incident & Adverse Event / Serious Occurrence analysis	35%	Transfer to Value Stream Coach and Department Managers	**Position eliminated and redistributed among Education, Research, Risk Management and Department Managers.**					
		B	Oversees Implementation of ROPS for Accreditation	15%	Transfer to Value Stream Coach and Department Managers						
		C	Assist with Claims Management	5%	Transfer to Risk Management						
		D	Education and training provision to staff, management, senior leaders, Board re: Patient Safety	10%	Transfer to Education						
		E	Review REDS electronic incident reports	15%	Transfer to Research						
		F	Committee Representation to provide patient safety perspective	20%	Transfer to Risk Management						
			Total	100%							
Quality Improvement Manager	2	A	Quality Improvement / Quality Improvement Plan (QIP)	25%	Part of E	Quality and Process Innovation Facilitator	2	A	Facilitating Process Improvement Workshops / Meetings	20%	
		B	Accreditation	25%	Moved to Accrediation, Policy and Forms Coordinator			B	Coaching and Mentorship	30%	New Responsibility
		C	Implementation of ROPs for Accreditation	12.5%	Implementation of ROPs is moved to Accrediation, Policy and Forms Coordinator.			C	Change Management	20%	New Responsibility
		D	Patient Experience / Quality Improvement Support / QI Committees	12.5%	Part of A, D, F			D	Improvement Projects/Initiatives Management	10%	
		E	Orientation/PR/Committee Representation	12.5%	May not be required in new structure.			E	Managing Internal / External Mandates	10%	
		F	Critical Incident and Serious Occurrence Follow Up, Review and Analysis / REDS review	12.5%	Transfer to Risk Management, Research, Value Stream Coordinator, and Department Managers			F	Patient / Family / Community Engagement	10%	
			Total	100.0%					**Total**	100%	
Forms Support Officer	1	A	Forms Management Process - Hospital Wide	70%	Part of D	Accreditation, Policies and Forms Support Officer	1	A	Facilitating Process Improvements / Meetings	10%	New Responsibility
		B	Committees	10%	Part of A			B	Coaching and Mentorship	10%	New Responsibility
		C	Forms Design (Forms Fast) and Intranet	10%	Part of D			C	Change Management	10%	New Responsibility
		D	Chart Packages / Volunteers	5%	Part of D			D	Initiatives Management	55%	Accreditation and Policies added
		E	General Office Duties	5%	Included in A to E			E	Managing Internal / External Mandates	15%	New Responsibility
			Total	100%					**Total**	100%	
Policy Coordinator	1	A	Policy and Forms Approval Process	35%	Part of A & D	Accreditation, Policies and Forms Coordinator	1	A	Facilitating Process Improvements / Meetings	15%	New Responsibility
		B	Policy Access	10%	Part of A & D			B	Coaching and Mentorship	15%	New Responsibility
		C	Consolidating policies from legacy organizations (policy library clean up)	25%	Part of D			C	Change Management	15%	New Responsibility
		D	Supervising Policy Department Staff	20%	Part of D			D	Initiatives Management	35%	Accreditation added
		E	Communicating Policy and Forms process changes to all staff	10%	Part of D			E	Managing Internal / External Mandates	20%	New Responsibility
			Total	100%					**Total**	100%	
Clerk, PMO	1	A	Project File Documentation Management	40%	Part of B & C	Program Assistant	1	A	General Administrative	40%	
		B	Administrative Duties	30%	Part of A			B	Process Improvement Initiatives Support	40%	
		C	Reception	15%	Part of A			C	Managing Internal / External Mandates	20%	
		D	FIPPA Lead	5%	Part of C						
		E	Project Financial Support	10%	Part of B						
			Total	100%					**Total**	100%	
Project Manager	5	A	Project planning	50%	Part of A, D & E	Project Manager	3	A	Facilitating Process Improvement Workshops / Meetings	20%	Revised focus
		B	Project Execution	20%	Part of A, D & E			B	Coaching and Mentorship	10%	New Responsibility
		C	Project Quality / Monitoring	10%	Part of D			C	Change Management	20%	New Responsibility
		D	Project Closure / Operationalization	10%	Part of D			D	Improvement Projects/Initiatives Management	30%	
		E	Portfolio Management	10%	Part of A, D & E			E	Managing Internal / External Mandates	10%	
								F	Patient / Family / Community Engagement	10%	New Responsibility
			Total	100%					**Total**	100%	

individual is expected to spend on that category of responsibility. On the right side of the template, fill in the same fields as above, but this time do so with the future state in mind. This helps in identifying overlaps and missed opportunities in the new job description created.

A real application of the above template at Hospital Heal reflecting sample job positions is shown in Table 7.2.

Once all the adjustments have been made and the categories of responsibilities finalized, detail the activities under the respective categories to create a job description for the position.

At Hospital Heal, job descriptions were created for all individuals who were part of the centralized core team, performance management, and decentralized team of value stream coaches that supported the operational teams to implement management system elements (discussed in Chapter 16) and other improvement initiatives. Given below is a sample job description for a value stream coach developed at Hospital Heal.

PURPOSE OF THE POSITION

The value stream coach is a high-profile role for a defined period of thirty months in which the successful incumbent participates in a "graduate" program with the intent of being absorbed into a suitable operational/administrative role within the organization once the assignment has been completed. During the initial six months of this period, the individual will receive education in lean management, lean thinking, project facilitation, project management, researching best practices, data analysis, critical incident management and audit, risk assessment and evaluation, patient/family engagement, accreditation, policy and forms, and communication management.

This individual works with the respective functional teams to support quality improvement initiatives under the philosophy of More Time to Care and in alignment with the Strategic Plan. The individual works collaboratively with the senior leadership team, physicians, psychologists, programs, and service leaders/teams among others in making successful transformational changes by facilitating group discussions; by analyzing current business process and work flows; by identifying opportunities for improvement; and by designing, developing, testing, and implementing change ideas through the application of leading-edge quality improvement strategies and techniques.

KEY ACTIVITIES AND RESPONSIBILITIES AND APPROXIMATE PERCENT OF TIME:

A. Facilitating process improvement sessions/meetings: 20%
- Conduct current state value steam/process mapping workshops to identify opportunities for improvement.
- Analyze current business process and workflows.
- Brainstorm ideas from teams to develop countermeasures for overcoming issues in the existing process.
- Review adverse events/near misses. Make recommendations to mitigate risk, enhance safety, improve quality, and ensure implementation of recommendations.
- Leverage domain expertise from process owners to develop innovative solutions for workflow optimization.
- Develop, pilot, implement, and sustain new processes.

B. Coaching and mentorship: 20%
- Align and prioritize projects with strategic directions.
- Educate teams to develop the problem statement. Establish project metrics and project charter.
- Support teams through knowledge transfer on the application of Lean/project management tools.
- Support teams through knowledge transfer on the application of Lean/patient and family–centered care tools.
- Develop standard work.

C. Change management: 20%
- Manage complex relationships with sponsors and stakeholders.
- Develop effective communication plans to manage stakeholder expectations.
- Educate teams on benefits of Lean management.
- Encourage and implement standard work.
- Develop a problem-solving culture based on data and best practices across the organization.
- Encourage and recognize contributions from teams and celebrate their learnings.

D. Improvement projects/initiatives management: 15%
- Provide leadership support to quality and process innovation facilitators and project managers.

- Successfully deliver complex, multiphased, multidisciplinary projects by balancing scope, time, cost, and quality.
- Design, develop, test, and implement change ideas using the Lean philosophy.
- Manage multiple projects to completion.
- Develop dashboards for internal and external report-outs.
- Maintain inventory of improvement initiatives in knowledge database.

E. Managing internal/external mandates: 10%
- Audit ROPs (required organizational practices) for accreditation to ensure compliance and measure for improvement.
- Manage expectations of internal mandates such as reporting to the board of directors and senior leadership team.
- Manage expectations of external mandates such as ministry, primary healthcare bodies, and other providers.
- Develop, implement, and manage policies and forms where required.

F. Patient/family/community engagement: 15%
- Capture voice of patient/family/community to increase understanding on the need for change.
- Ensure all processes are examined from the patient lens.
- Foster and maintain community partnerships.
- Engage community partners to improve access and flow.
- Implement processes to support a patient and family–partnered care environment.
- Develop, implement, coordinate, and evaluate engagement strategies for patients and families.

Sensei Gyaan: *Don't rush while developing this foundational component or else it will come back to bite you later, severely. Create an instrument that provides clarity, is robust enough to avoid overlap and confusion, and at the same time is agile enough to meet the evolving need of the business.*

Chapter 8

Develop the Recruitment Criteria and Select the Change Facilitators

There are three types of people in this world: those that make things happen, those who watch things happen and those who wonder what happened.

—Mary Kay Ash

Once the job descriptions are ready, you need to develop recruitment criteria, internal and external job postings, and an advertising plan to attract the right talent. Then you must design the interview and selection process. Design a process that tests candidates not only on their experience, knowledge, and skills, but also on their attitudes and behaviors. In the words of Tom Peters, "Hire for attitude. Train for skills." Use scenarios, simulations, and/or personality tests to select the candidate who is expected to be a superior cultural fit. A poor culture fit due to turnover can cost an organization between 50%–60% of the person's annual salary.

At Hospital Heal, a rigorous hiring process was implemented to select core team members and value stream coaches who had an excellent combination of technical talent and soft skills. To give you a sense of rigor, the six value stream coaches were selected among 182 applicants (Figure 8.1). Candidates who passed the initial screening went through a creative-problem-solving profiling exercise, a presentation based on a case scenario, an interview comprising situational behavioral questions, and a 360-degree recommendation check before

Figure 8.1 Six value stream coaches at Hospital Heal.

being offered the position. A similar process was conducted for selecting the members of the central core team to support continuous quality improvement, project management office, patient and family–partnered care, education, professional practice, knowledge management, accreditation, organizational policies, procedures, patient safety, and risk management. Positions that were not filled by internal candidates were posted on external job sites to hire the right candidate and ensure that the selection criteria were not compromised.

Given below is a sample candidate profile requirement for a value stream coach.

POSITION PREREQUISITES:

Required Qualifications:

■ Must be highly versatile, energized, and self-motivated
■ Demonstrated ability to influence and negotiate at all levels, internal and external to the organization
■ Demonstrated leadership, change-management, problem-solving, critical-thinking, conflict-resolution, team-building, and communication skills

- Must be able to support and contribute to a culture of safety and prevention of adverse health events in our organization
- Intermediate/advanced knowledge of Microsoft Word, PowerPoint, and Excel
- Good attendance and work record
- Criminal reference verification (recent as of three months)

Specific Certificates:

- A bachelor's degree in health, administration, health planning, or business administration, and/or equivalent education and experience, including clinical, with a minimum of five (5) years in a health-care environment.

DESIRABLE QUALIFICATIONS (ASSETS):

- Experience, knowledge, and active involvement in leading/implementing quality improvement initiatives/projects are an asset.
- Certification in Lean/Six Sigma/PMP is an asset.
- Bilingualism (English/French) is an asset.

Sensei Gyaan: A full time dedicated resource assigned for supporting continuous improvement projects has a capacity to simultaneously facilitate 8 projects or alternatively lead 4 projects, provided each project is scoped well to complete between 4–6 months. Use this formula as a rule of thumb for resource and budget allocation.

Chapter 9

Organize Visits to Best Practice Organizations for Leaders to "Go See Learn"

I'll go anywhere as long as it's forward.

—David Livingstone

Seeing is believing. Toyota promoted this concept by asking managers to "Go to Gemba," which in Japanese means to go to the actual place of work where value is created. Taiichi Ohno, an executive at Toyota, led the development of the concept of the Gemba walk. Gemba walks denote the action of going to see the actual process, understand the work, ask questions, and learn. The Gemba walk is an opportunity for staff to stand back from their day-to-day tasks to walk the floor of their workplace to identify wasteful activities. Gemba walk is designed to allow leaders to identify existing safety hazards, observe machinery and equipment conditions, ask about the practice standards, gain knowledge about the work status, and build relationships with employees. The objective of a Gemba walk is to understand the value stream and its problems rather than review results or make superficial comments. Dara Khosrowshahi, CEO of Uber says, "The thing I've found in life is that the higher up you get in an organization the less you know about what's going on."

Promoting the same philosophy, "Go See Learn" was coined at Hospital Heal, where the operational leaders and the senior executives were encouraged to move out of their offices and go to different areas across the hospital; meet with staff and patients; and observe, listen, and learn about their work. Ask questions to verify, clarify, or amplify (learn more about) your understanding. Remember that curiosity and judgment cannot occupy the same place at the same time. Stretching the concept of Go See Learn further, it meant to go, see, and learn from the experiences of other organizations who had been on the lean path for a long time. As they say, "If you want to be a lion, train yourself with lions."

Given below are examples of select few healthcare organizations that lean practitioners benchmark to demonstrate how maturity in lean application develops a culture of excellence.

- Cleveland Clinic
- Denver Health
- Flinders Hospital
- Kaiser Permanente
- Mayo Clinic
- NHS Bolton Trust
- NHS Western Sussex Hospital
- Park Nicollet Health Services
- Seattle Children's Hospital
- St. Boniface Hospital
- ThedaCare
- Virginia Mason Medical Centre

Hospital Heal arranged site visits to ThedaCare in Appleton, Wisconsin, one of the pioneers in implementing Lean in healthcare, for senior leaders, physicians, directors, and select managers to create buy-in on the transformational journey (Figure 9.1). Subsequently, site visits were organized for the

Figure 9.1   **Teams at Hospital Heal Go See Learn from ThedaCare, Wisconsin, USA.**

core team and value stream coaches to Go See Learn from other hospitals in the United States and Canada that were regarded as leaders in practicing patient-centered care, lean management, risk management, electronic medical administration record systems, etc.

Sensei Gyaan: *Bring back the concepts and learning from your visits and customize them to support your organization's culture. Don't expect to replicate success through copy and paste.*

MAKE CHANGE LAST

Chapter 10

Develop the Organization Report Card

Strategy is a commodity, execution is an art.

—Peter Drucker

According to a recent McKinsey survey, transformations with clear, unambiguous metrics and milestones were over seven times more likely to succeed than those lacking such elements.

In Chapter 4, I talked about the importance of integrating business excellence into an organization's strategic plan. In Chapter 5, I shared a model to integrate an organization's desired culture with strategy. With the strategic plan created, the task now at hand is to deploy the strategy throughout the organization from the boardroom to the frontline, as well as to monitor performance in relation to the strategic directions.

While there are many frameworks to deploy organization strategy, the popular ones include Balanced Scorecard (BSC) and Hoshin Kanri. The Balanced Scorecard's four perspectives, namely, financial, customer, process, and learning and growth, are comparable to Hoshin Kanri's cost, quality, delivery, and education (CQDE). Between the two, I prefer the Balanced Scorecard methodology for two reasons: one, the terminology of the four perspectives resonates well with organization strategy, and two, it is easier to understand and communicate to the frontline than the X Matrix used in Hoshin Kanri (Figure 10.1).

Let me explain the methodology for strategy deployment through a real case implementation. Hospital Heal used the BSC framework for strategy

Figure 10.1 The logic of the Balanced Scorecard.

deployment since the four strategic directions of its new strategic plan aligned more closely with the four perspectives of the BSC. The strategic deployment at Hospital Heal was undertaken in two steps:

1. Organization strategy cascaded to develop the hospital's "Health Report Card."
2. Hospital Report Card cascaded to develop department-level performance scorecards.

In this chapter, I will only focus on the first part, i.e., the process implemented for cascading the organization strategy to develop the hospital's Health Report Card, which was completed in a period of twelve weeks. The following activities were undertaken in the sequence listed below:

- Twenty hospitals across Canada in various stages of implementing Lean were randomly selected to understand the metrics they used for public reporting on their website (Figure 10.2).
- Malcolm Baldrige award winners in U.S. healthcare were approached to learn about metrics chosen by them for measuring organizational performance.
- Industry research was conducted on metrics used by the Canadian Institute for Health Information (CIHI).

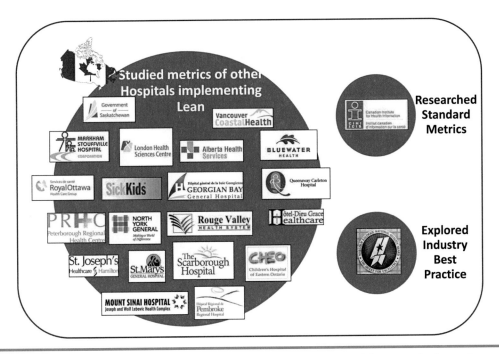

Figure 10.2   **Metric selection for creating Health Report Card for Hospital Heal.**

- Internal teams brainstormed possible metrics to support all twenty objectives of the new strategic plan.
- Inputs were sought from the senior leadership team on key process and outcome metrics.
- The hospital board approved the final metrics chosen for the report card.
- A detailed metric sheet was developed to outline the formula, definition, data owner, baseline, and target, all in layperson terms, to support each metric on the report card.
- An attractive, easy-to-understand layout of the Health Report Card was designed.
- A web portal for posting the Report Card for sharing with the general public was developed.
- Finally, the Report Card was published on the intranet and the hospital's website.

Sensei Gyaan: *Be very selective in terms of choosing the metrics for the organizational report card. Keep the key metrics to a manageable number of sixteen or less. Identify a mix of process and outcome metrics that are critical to quality, cost, delivery, safety, and morale.*

Chapter 11

Develop a Visual Strategy Room

Leadership is the art of giving people a platform for spreading ideas that work.

—Seth Godin

Once the organization report card is developed, the next step is to create a dedicated strategy room using the principles of visual management for the senior executives to strategize and reflect as a team on the performance of the organization. A dedicated strategy room that is used religiously by the senior executives and made accessible to all staff builds accountability, ownership, transparency, and teamwork. It also sends a message to the people that the organization strategy is a live document and not something that sits on the shelf or is discussed behind closed doors in a boardroom by the senior executive team.

The layout of the strategy room, the purpose and the flow of communication on each wall, the ease of understanding, the visual appeal, and the availability of standard work to read and interpret the work depicted on the walls are all factors that contribute to the success of how often and how effectively the room will be used by everyone. Else, it will become a modern art display room, where everyone appreciates the art but no one understands anything, nor do they see themselves as a part of it.

Given below is a concept of a visual strategy room, sometimes also called a "war room." The room is organized into four walls, with each wall having a distinct purpose (Figure 11.1). Availability of standard work ensures that everyone speaks the same language.

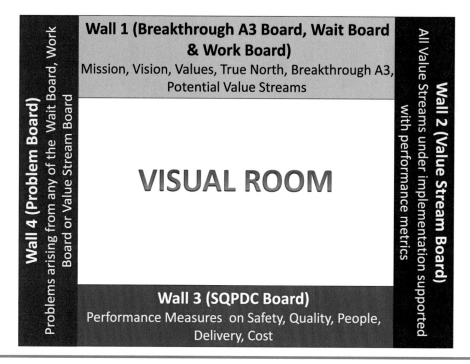

Figure 11.1 **The concept of a visual strategy room.**

- Wall 1 has the "true north" measures for the organization, breakthrough A3s, and potential value streams.
- Wall 2 has all the value streams under implementation supported with performance metrics.
- Wall 3 has the performance measures broken down on the basis of safety, quality, people, delivery, and cost.
- Wall 4 has all the problems arising from any of the other three walls that needs senior management's attention.

Based on the above concept, Hospital Heal customized their visual strategy room (Figure 11.2).

- Wall 1 had the key measures that the organization wanted to focus on for the one year in context.
- Wall 2 had the metrics the organization wanted to keep an eye on.
- Wall 3 had the projects in progress that supported the organization's priorities based on the metrics on Wall 1.
- Wall 4 informed the senior leadership team where support was required and highlighted celebrations.

WALL 1

	Organization Report Card		Driver Metrics				
Mission	Strategic Direction 1	Strategic Direction 2	Service Level	Strategic Direction 1	Strategic Direction 2	Strategic Direction 3	Strategic Direction 4
Vision			Clinical Services				
	Strategic Direction 3	Strategic Direction 4	Mental Health and Addiction Services				
Values			Corporate Services				

WALL 2

	Watch Metrics				Build Foundation For
Service Level	Strategic Direction 1	Strategic Direction 2	Strategic Direction 3	Strategic Direction 4	
Clinical Services					
Mental Health and Addiction Services					
Corporate Services					

WALL 3

	How are we doing - Clinical				How are we doing - Mental Health and Addictions				How are we doing - Corporate			
Status	SD 1	SD 2	SD 3	SD 4	SD 1	SD 2	SD 3	SD 4	SD 1	SD 2	SD 3	SD 4
Completed												
Work in Progress												
Waiting												

WALL 4

How can we help				Celebrations			
SD 1	SD 2	SD 3	SD 4	SD 1	SD 2	SD 3	SD 4

Figure 11.2 **Teams discussing projects in Hospital Heal's strategy room.**

The visual strategy room was open to all staff at the Hospital Heal. The CEO and the vice presidents reviewed Wall 4 during their weekly meetings and addressed any operational issues that were reflected on this wall. The directors met with the CEO and vice presidents on a quarterly basis to review the projects listed on Wall 3 and validated the priorities for the ongoing projects. Oftentimes, the directors brought their managers into the room to discuss the progress of the projects in their areas directly impacting Wall 1 and/or Wall 2, if their teams were currently building foundation for something long term. The value stream coaches conducted tours in batches of 12–15 for existing and new employees and walked them through all the four walls, not only to share how the information flowed between the walls, but also to acknowledge how the work of all employees supported the organization report card. The availability of standard work ensured that everyone spoke the same language.

The standard work created at Hospital Heal for conducting a visual room tour is shared below.

Standard Work for the Visual Strategy Room Tour			
Last Updated:		**Performed By:**	Senior leadership team, directors, performance excellence team
Revision:		**Frequency:**	As scheduled
Standard Work Owner:	Vice presidents and CEO	**Duration:**	15–30 minutes

Standard Work Purpose: The purpose of the visual room tour is to help participants understand how the organization cascades its priorities, identifies projects, completes work, and celebrates accomplishments.

PLAN

Prepare for the Visual Room Tour

Know your audience and the purpose of the tour. Tailor your presentation accordingly. Book the visual strategy room.

DO

1. Introduce yourself, welcome guests, and provide a Visual Strategy Room overview

- The visual room is where the CEO and the vice presidents gather regularly to strategize and reflect as a team on the performance of the organization. The information in the visual room has been organized into four walls, with each wall having a distinct purpose.
- Wall 1 has the key measures that the organization wants to focus on for the year.
- Wall 2 has the metrics the organization wants to keep an eye on.
- Wall 3 has the projects in progress that support the organization's priorities.
- Wall 4 informs the senior leadership team where support is required and highlights celebrations.

2. Explain the components of WALL 1

- Wall 1 is the strategy wall that includes the mission, vision, values, strategic directions, and associated metrics at the organization level for clinical services, mental health, addictions, senior's services, and corporate and support services.
- The Organization Report Card keeps us focused on achieving the milestones that we have set out in our strategic plan and identifies the areas where work is needed.
- The Report Card has been cascaded to service-level metrics, for which each vice president is accountable.
- The driver metrics drive performance at the organization, service, and department levels. These metrics are actively being worked on and may have an associated project.

(Continued)

3. **Explain the components of WALL 2**
• Wall 2 includes metrics that we do not want to lose sight of and items we are building our foundation on for this year. • Watch metrics are not being actively worked on and do not have any associated projects.
4. **Explain the components of WALL 3**
• Wall 3 displays project status updates by service level. • Make the connection between the projects under the "work in progress" category and the metrics on Wall 1. • Through prioritization, some projects/initiatives are categorized as "waiting" and will start when organizational capacity allows. • The row on implemented projects/initiatives shows projects that have been completed.
5. **Explain the components of WALL 4**
• Wall 4 contains issues that require assistance or that have been escalated for support. It also includes celebrations. • Share a recent celebration.
STUDY
Share and discuss your learning and observations from the visual room tour with your colleagues during huddles, monthly scorecard reviews, or visual room performance reviews.
ADJUST
Through experimentation and interactions, your own learning will begin to influence the visual room tour.

The ongoing senior leadership commitment to demonstrate the use of the visual strategy room supported by a formal governance structure of weekly, monthly, and quarterly meetings to discuss the information on the walls, built accountability at all levels and brought focus to the key priorities of Hospital Heal.

Sensei Gyaan: *While the primary audience for the strategy room is the senior executives, encourage leaders at all levels of the organization to review the room with their respective teams on a regular basis and relate how their work contributes to moving the big dot measures of the organization.*

Chapter 12

Develop the Process to Cascade the Organization Strategy to the Frontline

If you can't fly then run, if you can't run then walk, if you can't walk then crawl, but whatever you do you have to keep moving forward.

—Martin Luther King, Jr.

In Chapter 10, I shared the first step of the two-step process of cascading the organization strategy. In this chapter, I will talk about the second step of the process for cascading the organization report card to develop performance scorecards for all areas of the organization.

Let's continue to learn from the example of Hospital Heal. The hospital's new strategic plan reflected five strategic objectives under each of its four strategic directions. The sheer magnitude of the work required to deploy the strategy with twenty objectives across the organization was daunting. The challenge was to ensure that the frontline team understood how their work impacted these strategic objectives (Figure 12.1).

Hospital Heal developed a unique and innovative approach to engage the frontline staff and cascaded its hospital report card to all areas across the organization. It was done in the following two stages:

Figure 12.1   **Hospital Heal's approach to cascading strategy.**

1. Preparation for cascading the hospital's Health Report Card: completed in six weeks
2. Actual development of performance scorecards for all areas across the hospital: completed in three weeks

Activities undertaken during the preparation stage included the following:

- Over 300 metrics were brainstormed to support all areas across the hospital, covering mental health, physical health, and corporate services.
- Six mandatory metrics were selected that would be used by every scorecard area
- A standard approach and educational materials were developed to support cascading of the Health Report Card.
- Twelve individuals were trained to facilitate teams during workshops for developing performance scorecards.
- Awareness sessions on the Balanced Scorecard philosophy and the approach to develop area-specific performance scorecards during the forthcoming workshops were conducted for all teams across the organization (Figures 12.2 and 12.3).
- Blog posts and one-page handouts on performance scorecard were created and shared to engage the frontline and their supervisors.
- Eighty areas were identified that needed to be represented on a performance scorecard.
- Working group representatives from each of the eighty areas were selected. The team composition included members at all levels: frontline, supervisors, managers, and directors.

Figure 12.2 **Education sessions conducted at Hospital Heal for developing scorecards.**

Activities undertaken to develop performance scorecards included the following:

■ Eighty working groups were facilitated by twelve individuals (six core team members and six value stream coaches) to develop their respective performance scorecards. Depending upon the size and the complexity of their area, each group required between one and three half-day workshop sessions to complete their respective scorecard.

Figure 12.3 **Facilitators promoting development of scorecards at Hospital Heal.**

Table 12.1   Template Used at Hospital Heal for Developing Performance Scorecards

Strategic Direction	Strategic Objective	Service Level Metric	Department Metric	Formula for calculating metric	Frequency of measure	Metric Reporting Owner	Baseline	Target

- In addition to the six mandatory metrics provided, each team selected an additional six area-specific metrics. Each scorecard had a minimum of six and a maximum of twelve metrics (Table 12.1).
- All eighty performance scorecards were reviewed by their respective director and approved by their respective vice president (Figure 12.4).

Once the process was tested for two years, a standard work process was developed at Hospital Heal to create their annual report card. This process is shared in Table 12.2.

Figure 12.4   Breakdown of scorecards by area.

Table 12.2 Standard Work Process for Developing Annual Report Card for Hospital Heal

Process	Review strategy plan to confirm it meets Operational needs	Quality and Risk Working Group review different sources to prepare metrics for Report Card	Senior Leadership Team establishes Hospital Report Card metrics for the fiscal year	Quality Committee of the Board approves QIP indicators for the fiscal year	Board approves Hospital Report Card	Update the Hospital Report Card
Tasks Associated with the Process Steps	SLT reviews and confirms for the next fiscal: • Vision • Strategic Directions • Strategic Objectives • Driver Objectives • Watch Objectives • Board confirms direction for the next fiscal	VPs provide input on metrics and targets pertaining to their respective area using some or all of the following sources to support the decision on metrics: • Quality Improvement Plan (QIP) • Quality Based Procedures (QBPs) • Accreditation and Risk reports • Industry benchmarking • Master programming • Performance based on previous years Report Card • New mandates provided by Ministry • Infrastructure changes planned • Discussions and agreements with our partners etc. • Determine data leads and metric owners	VPs and CEO collectively review and finalize: • Metrics for the Report Card • QIP metrics associated with executive compensation	Quality Committee of the Board: • Approves Corporate Report Card metrics associated with QIP indicators for next year • Reviews QIP Progress Report last year • Review QIP narrative and indicators associated with Executive Compensation Develop metric sheet for each measure chosen for the Report Card • Define the metric • Establish formula for calculating the metric • Establish baseline and target	As regards QIP, Board of Directors: • Approves Corporate Report Card metrics associated with QIP indicators for next year • Reviews QIP Progress Report last year • Review QIP narrative and indicators associated with Executive Compensation • Board of Directors reviews and accepts Hospital Report Card • Performance Management Team updates new metrics on Report Card Template and arranges for French translation • Communication Team posts Report Card and metric sheets internally and externally on the websites	• Metric Leads contacted to update the metric sheets • Report card is updated on the websites • Visual Room is updated with the quarterly metrics
Process Step Coordinated by	Quality and Performance Excellence	Quality and Performance Excellence	Quality and Performance Excellence	Performance Management	Performance Management	Performance Management
Completion Timeline	November	December	January	February	March	Quarterly

Sensei Gyaan: *Select no more than five metrics per scorecard area (three mandatory and two area specific). Upon reflection in the following year at Hospital Heal, the number of mandatory metrics was reduced to five, as hospital management realized that twelve metrics were too many for teams to manage in any given year.*

Chapter 13

Develop Project Prioritization and Selection Criteria

Desires dictate our priorities, priorities shape our choices, and choices determine our actions.

—Dallin H. Oaks

Once the performance scorecards have been developed for all areas in the organization, teams brainstorm ideas to identify projects and initiatives to be undertaken for achieving measures chosen in their scorecards. In the enthusiasm to achieve the objectives of their new scorecards, the number of project ideas quickly adds up. Suddenly it becomes overwhelming for teams to prioritize and select the ones they should implement. Most organizations regularly struggle with this problem as they are challenged with limited resource availability.

In Chapters 13 and 14 I will share, through a real case example, how to create and use a standard prioritization and project selection criteria that provide equity across all areas to allocate manpower and financial resources for implementing projects. The process ensures that the projects implemented in different areas are aligned to positively impact the big dot measures at the organization level.

Problem: *The inventory of all projects, big and small across Hospital Heal, stood at a staggering count of 634. Every project was deemed important. The other challenge was that the criteria for project selection varied among teams* *and there was little clarity on the impact the project had on other functional areas or on the overall performance of the organization.*

Solution: *Senior Executive team and council members of More Time to Care, who represented all critical areas of the hospital, discussed and agreed to standardize classification of all projects using the PICK chart triaging process (Figures 13.1 and 13.2). The following three project categories were standardized (visually represented in Figure 13.3):*

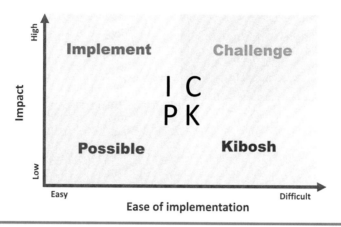

Figure 13.1   PICK chart for triaging ideas generated.

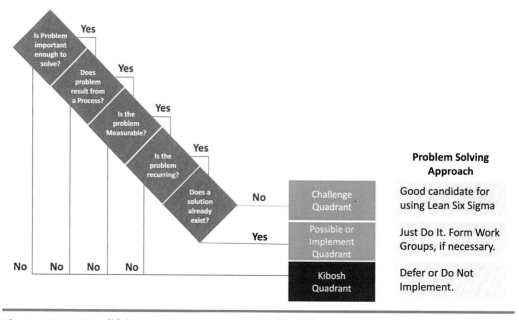

Figure 13.2   Qualifying projects in the PICK chart quadrants.

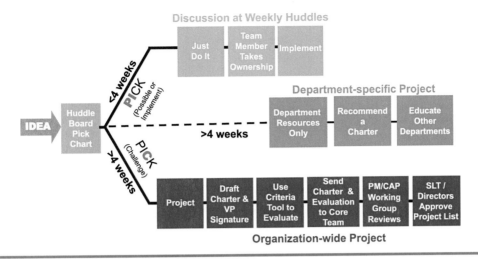

Figure 13.3 **Project classification criteria developed at Hospital Heal.**

Project Classification

- **Just do it (JDI):** Part of incremental change, where an individual or a small working group within a local area comes together to implement the improvement idea in less than four weeks.
- **Continuous-improvement project (CI):** Part of transitional change that requires more than four weeks but less than six months to implement. This type of project needs a charter to be developed and resources to be assigned for implementation. The project may impact one or more functional areas but does not require any capital investment approval from the financial committee.

Table 13.1 **Example of Filters Under Benefit and Effort**

Project Idea		BENEFIT							EFFORT					VALUE	
		Financial Return on Investment (ROI)	Increases Reliability/ Quality	Improves Efficiency	Reduces Lead Time	Improves Customer Experience	Increases Employee Engagement	Total Benefit	Capital Investment Required	Time required to complete the project	Resource Requirement	Risk of failure	Total Effort	Total Benefit/ Total Effort	Priority
	Weightage	20%	25%	15%	20%	25%	15%	100%	10%	25%	15%	30%	100%		
1															
2															
3															
4															
5															

Table 13.2 Example of Filters and Their Operational Definitions for Project Evaluation

Financial Return on Investment (ROI)	Increases Reliability/ Quality	Improves Efficiency	Reduces Lead Time	Improves Customer Experience	Increases Employee Engagement	Requires Capital Investment	Time required to complete the project	Resource Requirement	Risk of failure
High = 5 Medium = 3 Low = 1 Not Applicable = 0	High = 5 Medium = 3 Low = 1 Not Applicable = 0	High = 5 Medium = 3 Low = 1 Not Applicable = 0	High = 5 Medium = 3 Low = 1 Not Applicable = 0	High = 5 Medium = 3 Low = 1 Not Applicable = 0	High = 5 Medium = 3 Low = 1 Not Applicable = 0	High = 1 Medium = 3 Low = 5 Not Applicable = 0	High = 1 Medium = 3 Low = 5 Not Applicable = 0	High = 1 Medium = 3 Low = 5 Not Applicable = 0	High = 1 Medium = 3 Low = 5 Not Applicable = 0
5: ROI<= 3 years (3 yr Capital Costs + 3 yr Operational Costs < 3 yr support Costs + 3 yr Savings Achieved)	5: Increases Reliability/ Quality by >=90%	5: Impact >=20%	5: Reduces Lead Time by >=50%	5: Reduces customer travel distance to <=5 kms	5: Increases Employee Engagement score by >=10%	1: Capital investment required >=$25K per annum	1: Time to completion is >=12 months	1: Additional manpower required >= 0.5FTE	1: Risk Index is HIGH
3: ROI is between 3-5 years	3: Increases Reliability/ Quality between 75-90%	3: Impact between 10-20%	3: Reduces Lead Time between 25-50%	3: Reduces customer travel distance between 5-10 kms	3: Increases Employee Engagement score between 5-10%	3: Capital Investment required between $0-25K	3: Time to completion is between 6 -12 months	3: Additional manpower required <= 0.5FTE	3: Risk Index is MEDIUM
1: ROI is between 5-10 years	1: Increases Reliability/ Quality by <=75%	1: Impact <=10%	1: Reduces Lead Time by <=25%	1: Reduces customer travel distance to <=10 km	1: Increases Employee Engagement score by 5%	5: Zero Capital Investment required	5: Time to completion is <=6 months	5: Zero additional FTE required	5: Risk index is LOW
0: No ROI/ No Relationship	0: No Impact/ No Relationship	0 = No Relationship/ No Impact on Efficiency	0 = No Impact/ No Relationship to Lead Time	0 = No Impact/ No Relationship to Customer Experience	0 = No Impact/ No Relationship to Employee Engagement	0 = No Relationship	0 = No Relationship	0 = No Relationship	0 = No Relationship

Table 13.3 Example of Poor Organizational Focus: 10 Filters with Equal Weights

Project Idea	Financial Return on Investment (ROI)	Increases Reliability/ Quality	Improves Efficiency	Reduces Lead Time	Improves Customer Experience	Increases Employee Engagement	Requires Capital Investment	Time required to complete the project	Resource Requirement	Risk of failure	Total Score	Priority
Weightage	10%	10%	10%	10%	10%	10%	10%	10%	10%	10%	100%	
1												
2												
3												
4												
5												

- **Organization-wide project:** Part of transitional change in which a project charter is developed, resources are allocated, and the change is implemented within a twelve-month period. Longer-duration projects are broken down into smaller, more manageable phases. The project typically impacts more than one functional area and needs capital investment approval from the financial committee.

Project Prioritization Criteria

Once the project fell under the continuous-improvement or organization-wide category, it had to compete against other projects to qualify for resource allocation. Filters (standardized criteria) for project selection were established, weights were provided for each criterion (total weights of all filters add to 100% as shown in Table 13.1). Each filter was defined at three levels—high, medium, and low—with the objective of creating value. Value was numerically defined as benefit divided by effort, which meant to increase the value you can either increase the numerator (benefit) or reduce the denominator (effort). For filters that contributed to increasing the numerator, the high was rated as 5 and the low was rated as 1. For filters that contributed to reducing the denominator, high was rated as 1 and the low was rated as 5. Operational definitions for criteria were created to prioritize projects across the organization. Examples of project filters and their operational definitions are shared in Table 13.2. The results of the solution are shared in the next chapter.

Sensei Gyaan: *Limit the total number of filters (benefit filters + effort filters) to a maximum of six. Avoid giving equal weights to all filters to reflect relative importance (Table 13.3). When choosing filters, do not identify filters that only increase the numerator (benefit). Give due consideration for identifying filters that also reduce the denominator (effort) to increase overall value.*

Chapter 14

Prioritize and Select the Critical Few Improvement Initiatives across the Organization

> *Everything that can be counted does not necessarily count; everything that counts cannot necessarily be counted.*
>
> **—Albert Einstein**

In Chapter 13, we learned how to categorize projects into JDI, CI, and organization-wide projects. We also learned about selecting filters (criteria) at an organization level, allocating a weight percentage to each filter, and creating operational definitions for the chosen filters. In this chapter, we will learn how to prioritize projects using these filters.

However, just before doing that, let us understand an important but often misunderstood concept: the difference between standard and standardization. Standard is a rule with no deviation (same as a policy), while standardization is a guiding standard that allows teams flexibility to adapt to it in their respective work areas. Cardiologist Robert Wilson, at ThedaCare, describes standard work as "flexible regimentation." Regimentation refers to developing a common or standard process for performing a specific service based on the best available evidence; flexible refers to ongoing efforts to improve the standard process. So, how do you deliver results when change

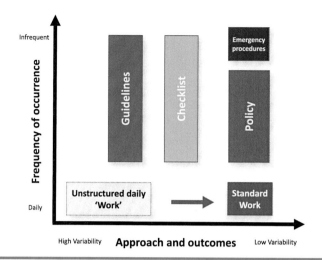

Figure 14.1 Differentiating standard work from policy and guidelines.

depends on people doing their work differently? You create and follow standard work (or a policy) where the failure to do so may lead to defects, part rejects, customer complaints, unacceptable service levels, or risk of harm to equipment, body, or life. In almost all other cases, Lean promotes standardized work, even though you most often hear or read "standard work" (Figure 14.1).

Another important Lean term that finds varied usage is the Japanese word "Kaizen"—some definitions translate it as "change for the better," while others loosely relate it to "Continuous Improvement." Jun Nakamuro, disciple of Taichi Ohno, in his article, "Re-Translating Lean from its Origin," defines "Kaizen" as "Self-Development," where individuals change their own actions to develop a new mindset. Toyota teaches their employees that they have two jobs: (1) Do their work (follow the standardized work) and (2) To improve their work ("Kaizen").

Richard Branson, chairman of the Virgin Group, says, "When I think about my life, routine isn't a word that naturally comes to mind. I love to be adventurous, I love to be unusual and I love to be spontaneous. I also spend a lot of my life on the move. So why would I need a routine? Nevertheless, I do have a routine, and I swear by it." As a leader, it is your duty to ask (1) Do we have standard work?, (2) Are we following standard work?, and (3) What is wrong with standard work if we are not following it?

Now, let's continue with our learning on prioritization. Teams across the organization are provided an option to either use the same weight percentage as assigned to the filters at the organizational level or use them as a

Table 14.1 **Project Prioritization Template**

Project Idea	Financial Return on Investment (ROI)	Increases Reliability/ Quality	Improves Efficiency	Improves Customer Experience	Time required to complete the project	Risk of failure	Total Score	Priority
Weightage	10	20	25	20	15	10	100	
Project 1	1	5	1	5	3	5	330	2
Project 2	5	1	0	0	1	3	115	4
Project 3	5	3	1	5	3	1	290	3
Project 4	3	3	5	5	3	1	370	1
Project 5	1	0	1	0	5	0	110	5

guideline, in which case teams customize weights to make them relevant to their respective work area. Note that the filters do not change, but the weights may. This allows flexibility to operate within the standard to create a better alignment between the team's functional area and the organizational strategy.

Once the filters and weights are agreed upon, the team lists all their project ideas in the project prioritization template (Table 14.1). All project ideas are required to pass through these filters and compete for resource allocation. Based on the operational definitions established (see Chapter 13), teams allocate ratings of 1, 3, 5, or 0 depending on each filter's association to the respective project. For computing the total score, multiply each rating with the respective weight of the filter and add them together. Once the total scores of all projects are computed, arrange the total score column in descending order, i.e., the project idea with the highest score goes to the top (ranked first) and a sequential project list in the order of priority is generated. The projects then receive resource allocation in that order.

Results: *The implementation of the above approach at Hospital Heal (Table 14.2) reduced the number of projects from 634 to 198 in the first attempt and then to 45 after a few more. All projects were completely aligned to the organization's Health Report Card and impacted the big dot measures of the organization.*

Table 14.2   **Project Prioritization Template Implemented at Hospital Heal**

| Department: |
| VP: |
| Director: |
| Manager: |

						Importance Rating Filters							
Access to Right Care Partnerships with Purpose Our People Achieving Their Best Wise Choices						Financial Integrity	Increases Efficiency	Improves Safety & Quality	Increase Access	Builds Partnerships Internal/External	Risk of not implementing the initatve		
STRATEGIC DIRECTION	STRATEGIC OBJECTIVE	INITIATIVE	METRIC	CURRENT PERFORMANCE	TARGET / GOAL	15%	20%	25%	20%	10%	10%	SCORE	RANK
		1											
		2											
		3											
		4											
		5											

Projects where a lead could be assigned without delay were initiated, while others were put in the project pipeline and scheduled as personnel became available. Projects that were mandated by the Ministry of Health and Long Term Care, that affected accreditation, that were infrastructure related, or that received special funding from the ministry were not prioritized using the standardized criteria tool. These projects received priority over other projects identified by the department (Figure 14.2).

Figure 14.2   **Teams reviewing and prioritizing projects at Hospital Heal.**

Sensei Gyaan: *Do not prioritize projects of the following categories along with projects in the general category. Sometimes these projects may not score as high as you may expect them to when compared to the general projects. The categories include*

1. *Projects that are mandated by any external body such as the government, accreditation office, environmental sustainability officials, or others*
2. *Special projects for which you have already received or expect to receive additional funding*
3. *Projects related to infrastructure or asset management, if not undertaken, may be a potential risk to business operations. Examples include annual maintenance of the building, equipment, hardware, or software or replacing old equipment, hardware, or software that is obsolete or in poor condition.*

Chapter 15

Define the Roles and Responsibilities of the Project Team

Winners practice till they get it right, Champions practice till they can't get it wrong.

—Anonymous

Once you have a list of projects prioritized, it is important that you develop a clear understanding of the roles and responsibilities of the individuals on the project team. This instills common language among the facilitators and also between the facilitators and the teams across the organization. The following role titles are commonly associated with a project team (Figure 15.1),

- **Sponsor:** Responsible for approving the project and its resources
- **Champion:** Responsible for results and assigning resources
- **Project lead:** Responsible for coordinating the project from start to finish
- **Process owner:** Subject matter expert (SME) on the process who provides information on best practices and can also assume the role of a project lead

Figure 15.1 **Role titles in a project team.**

- **Team member:** Responsible for contributing ideas and implementing the solution
- **Facilitator:** Responsible for methodology

While the above titles are standard practice in most organizations implementing Lean Six Sigma, the description of the roles and responsibilities within those tiles varies depending on the size and structure of the organization. In smaller organizations, often the roles overlap among sponsor, champion, and process owner. Even though the literature defines the responsibility of the process owner as the one who is fully responsible for the process performance, process maturity, process improvements, and performance of the resources in the process, it is recommended that the role of process owner be kept distinct from sponsor or champion.

Given below is an example of roles and responsibilities of the project team at Hospital Heal mapped onto the life cycle of a project (Table 15.1). Create a similar table of roles and responsibilities for implementing projects in your organization.

Table 15.1 Roles and Responsibilities of a Project Team at Hospital Heal

	Sponsor	Champion	Lead/Process Owner (Subject Matter Expert)	Facilitator	Team Member
Business Case		Creates business case for projects and/or rationale for continuous-improvement activities. Secures funding as required			
Initiating and Charter	Signs the high-level project charter, which commissions the project and provides authority to the champion and the facilitator to proceed to planning stage Arranges and approves resources where requested and deemed appropriate	Creates high-level' project charter in consultation with project facilitator and the team members of the project	Supports the creation of the 'high-level' project charter	Guides project team on charter development and ensures sponsor signs off on the agreement before work commences	Resource assigned by sponsor/ champion on the projects

(Continued)

Table 15.1 (Continued) Roles and Responsibilities of a Project Team at Hospital Heal

	Sponsor	Champion	Lead/Process Owner (Subject Matter Expert)	Facilitator	Team Member
Planning	Signs detailed project management plan prior to the execution of projects	Approves the project management plan	Collaborates with the facilitator, champion, and team members to create the project management plan	Guides the project team through the steps of project management processes, including all administrative requirements	Provides the project management plan
	Secures and approves any additional funding, where required	Participates in continuous improvement events and provides direction	Leads the continuous improvement events with support from the facilitator	Fosters a culture that promotes research and evaluation of best practices, and encourages experimentation	Participates in continuous-improvement events

(Continued)

Table 15.1 (Continued) Roles and Responsibilities of a Project Team at Hospital Heal

	Sponsor	Champion	Lead/Process Owner (Subject Matter Expert)	Facilitator	Team Member
Execution		Oversees project deliverables and is accountable for project outcomes	Directs and executes the project management plan with team members	Ensures project remains on track as per project toll gates and alerts lead when counter-measures are required	Executes the project management plan with direction from the lead and support from the facilitator
			Tracks and collects baseline and post-project measurements as required as an input into the sustainability plan and report-out documentation		Participates in collecting data as directed by the lead

(Continued)

Table 15.1 (*Continued*) Roles and Responsibilities of a Project Team at Hospital Heal

	Sponsor	Champion	Lead/Process Owner (Subject Matter Expert)	Facilitator	Team Member
Communication	Develops elevator speech for the project Reviews project updates in monthly performance scorecard review meeting	Provides project updates to sponsor during the monthly performance scorecard review meeting	Regularly meets with the facilitator and provides project updates to the sponsor and/or champion Communicates charter to team members	Provides regular status reports to the sponsor and champion as necessary Updates/coordinates with resource manager as required	
Issue Resolution	Demonstrates support for the project and removes any roadblocks impacting project health/milestones	Resolves issues presented by project lead or escalates issues to sponsor	Supports team members to resolve issues or obstacles Escalates unresolved issues to champion	Documents risks/issues and guides project team to a resolution prior to escalation	Escalates unresolved issues to project lead

(Continued)

Table 15.1 (*Continued*)   Roles and Responsibilities of a Project Team at Hospital Heal

	Sponsor	Champion	Lead/Process Owner (Subject Matter Expert)	Facilitator	Team Member
Closing/ Sustainabil- ity	Closes the project on completion based on the deliverables outlined in the charter	Approves sustain- ability plan	Creates sustainabil- ity plan for cham- pion approval	Notifies sponsor and team when project officially closes	Participates in sustainability activities
	Authorizes discon- tinuation of the project at any point by providing valid reasons	Approves and participates in project report-out	Devises report-out document, obtains champion approval, and schedules report- out with value stream coach		Participates in project report-outs

Sensei Gyaan: *If you have to choose between a process owner with high technical SME but low business SME and one with a high business SME but low technical SME, select the one with a high technical SME. Note that process owners are responsible for the efficiency and effectiveness of the process. To create effectiveness and efficiency in a process does not require the ability to manage the business covered by the process.*

Chapter 16

Define the Guiding Principles and Management System Elements to Sustain the Excellence Journey

Real improvement comes from changing systems, not from change within systems.

—Donald Berwick

Most organizations struggle to sustain change in their organization. Experience informs the following five reasons as the key contributors to failed cultural transformation journeys:

1. Behaviors expected from employees are not clearly articulated.
2. A conducive environment for employees to demonstrate expected behaviors on a daily basis is not provided.
3. The new way of working is not integrated into the employees' daily work.
4. The excellence journey is treated as a project/initiative.
5. Leadership's commitment to the excellence journey falters when the organization is in financial difficulty.

Since the control and sustain phases in most business excellence philosophies or project implementation frameworks are typically the last phases, not enough attention is given to developing countermeasures for the above causes in the earlier phases of the journey or while building the foundation for change. In the last ten years, enough evidence has been collected through studying and learning from successful organizations that what differentiates a top-performing organization with others is their *culture*.

In Chapter 5, we learned about culture, its constituents, and the role of leadership in developing organizational culture. In Chapter 6, we learned about business excellence models and their constituents. This chapter combines the lessons from Chapters 5 and 6 to create the management system framework required for developing a culture that delivers the new results an organization needs to achieve.

But first, let me clarify some terminology that leaders and practitioners find confusing. Figure 16.1 shows the different excellence terminologies mapped out on the seven categories of the best-practice Malcolm Baldrige framework, used for awarding U.S. organizations in the business, healthcare, education, and nonprofit sectors for performance excellence.

Organizations that achieve the performance excellence status align and integrate their leadership, strategy, customers, measurement, analysis and knowledge management, workforce, and operations to produce the best overall results. An organization can have excellent processes and products, but if its strategy is wrong or its results are poor, the organization will not achieve performance excellence. Don't confuse project results with organizational results. The key to performance/organizational excellence

Figure 16.1 **Excellence terminologies mapped onto the seven categories of a Malcolm Baldrige framework. (Adapted from Business Excellence Institute.)**

Figure 16.2　**Kumar Management System$^©$.**

is combining and managing all aspects of value creation in the business together, and establishing an internal framework of standards and processes to achieve and sustain outstanding levels of performance that meets or exceeds the expectations of all the stakeholders. Achieving operational excellence requires the successful implementation of a business strategy.

Since Baldrige looks at all components of an organization with equal emphasis and focuses on how each part impacts and links with the others, it provides a true systems perspective. It is for this reason that I have used the categories of the Baldrige model to create the Kumar Management System$^©$ (Figure 16.2).

How the Kumar Management System Works

The customers are at the top of the management system model. The customers truly guide the leadership in setting the direction and establishing organizational goals and strategy that include their voices, experiences, needs, and expectations. The strategy informs the area of focus and the corresponding big dot measures for the organization. The big dot measures inform the processes (operations) that need to be improved to achieve the overall organization strategy. The next step is to make sure that the people have the right skills and education to work on these processes. The desired operational metrics inform the skill gap that needs to be bridged in the workforce for delivering best-in-class performance. In the category of measurement, information, and knowledge management, a business constantly feeds and analyzes data and compares the data with not only the inputs and desired outcomes expected from all other categories, but also with external influences and benchmarks. The feedback loop informs us how well we are doing. It allows us to take corrective actions on a continual basis and adjust our areas of focus for the organization as a whole. The PDSA improvement cycle continues indefinitely in pursuit of achieving organizational excellence and culture transformation (results).

The Kumar Management System comprises fourteen guiding principles (Figure 16.3) and twenty-two sustenance elements (Figure 16.4) to support an organization on their journey to excellence and culture transformation. These principles and sustenance elements of the Kumar Management System have been handpicked after careful consideration (Figure 16.5) and are based on two decades of industry experience, practical lessons from visiting several leading best-practice organizations, and also extensive research on best-practice frameworks and methodologies such as Shingo, Malcolm Baldrige, Lean, Six Sigma, Patient-Centered Care, and Performance Management, among others.

A word of caution to readers: the elements of the management system are not tools. David Mann, in his book *Creating a Lean Culture*, states that a management system drives the culture of an organization by sustaining and extending the gains from implementing Lean improvements. Let me explain this through some practical examples. Visual management is a management system element. Examples of tools that support visual management include

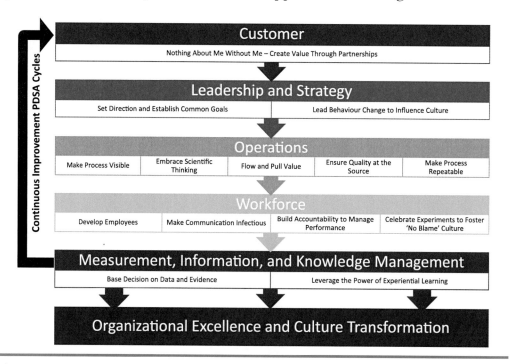

Figure 16.3 **Fourteen guiding principles of the Kumar Management System©.**

Figure 16.4   Twenty-two elements of the Kumar Management System©.

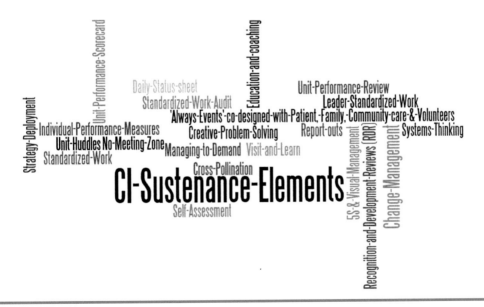

Figure 16.5   Partial list of potential elements in a management system.

5S, performance scorecard boards, and patient whiteboards. Likewise, the tools that supports Systems Thinking include the value stream map, systems map and an assets map; the tools such as the fishbone diagram, 5 Why analysis, A3 problem solving, challenge map, and KJ analysis support creativity and innovation; and the tools of staff conversation, customer/patient conversation, and process observation support the management system element of Go See Learn. While the tools are important, what is crucial is the need to ingrain management system elements into the fabric of daily operations to change the behavior of people, a key instrument in organizational transformation.

Validation of the Kumar Management System

The guiding principles and the sustenance elements of the Kumar Management System were validated at Hospital Heal while implementing their excellence journey of More Time to Care (Table 16.1 and Figure 16.6).

Table 16.1 Guiding Principles and Sustenance Elements Implemented at Hospital Heal

Category	#	Guiding Principles	#	CI Sustenence Elements
Patients	1	Nothing About Me Without Me - Create Value through partnerships	1	Patient and Family Partnered Care Practices
Leadership & Strategy	2	Set direction and establish common goals	2	Hospital Report Card
			3	Team Performance Scorecard
			4	Systems Thinking
	3	Lead behaviour change to influence culture	5	Change Management
Process	4	Make process visible	6	Visual Management
	5	Embrace Scientific Thinking	7	Team based Creative Problem Solving
	6	Flow and Pull Value	8	Managing to Demand
	7	Ensure Quality at the source	9	No Meeting Zone
			10	Go See and Learn
			11	Daily Status sheet
			12	Standard Work Observation
	8	Make process repeatable	13	Standard Work for key unit level processes
People	9	Develop employees	14	Education and Coaching
	10	Make communication infectious	15	Team Huddles
	11	Build accountability to manage performance	16	Individual Performance Measures
			17	Recognition and Development Reviews
			18	Leader Standard Work
	12	Celebrate Experiments to foster 'No Blame' culture	19	Team Report Outs
Measurement, Information and Knowledge Management	13	Base decision on data and evidence	20	Monthly Performance Scorecard Review
			21	Benchmarking and Reflection
	14	Leverage the power of experiential learning	22	Cross Pollination

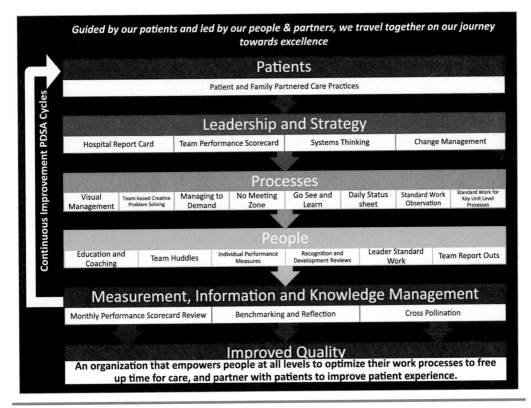

Figure 16.6 **Sustenance elements of the More Time to Care initiative implemented at Hospital Heal.**

Patient and Family–Partnered Care Practices

Now let me elaborate the category of patients, share the patient and family–partnered care practices, and provide the roadmap that was developed and implemented at Hospital Heal. But before that, I would like to share my story of the journey to creating the roadmap and some revelations of what I experienced along the way.

To understand and learn more about the patient and family–centered care practices, I went on a learning mission along with two members of my team. We visited several hospitals in Canada and the United States that are recognized as leaders in practicing patient and family–centered care. We read a lot of best-practice literature on patient-centered care. We participated in leading conferences focused on patient-centered care to learn from the experiences of other healthcare providers and consumers. We spoke to some of the senior leaders and key personnel who are respected in this field to seek their guidance for developing a roadmap to implement patient and family–centered care at a hospital. We also sat as observers in some of the advisory council meetings.

While there was immense learning and exposure to practices and experiences of others who had tread this path before, I was amazed that we could not get a compelling answer that could direct me with confidence about where to start and what potential practices to include while designing a roadmap to patient and family–partnered care. I understand that every journey is different and you cannot copy-paste someone else's journey to implement yours. However, I just hoped that I would have gotten a better response than "It depends." The only common ground that most hospitals or individuals shared was to have a patient advisory committee.

So, the only option left was to design a roadmap based on the knowledge gained during our learning mission and relate it to the culture of the organization. After several weeks of deliberation and consultations within Hospital Heal, we designed a customized roadmap built on the four key concepts of patient and family–centered care, namely, dignity and respect, information sharing, participation, and collaboration. The roadmap consisted of eight guiding principles and twenty-two associated patient and family–centered care practices (Table 16.2).

The irony is that the practice of having a patient advisory committee, which was universally recommended, was not implemented. Instead, a conscious decision was made to build a pool of patient volunteers, leverage their knowledge, and involve them by matching the right experience with the improvement project instead of having a few select patient advocates providing input on every change initiative. This collaborative approach with patients and families positively impacted the quality of input in all projects and also their deliverables. For that reason, the practice was strategically termed as "partnered care" instead of "centered care" to reflect true collaboration with patients and families for improving their health outcome.

Twelve out of the twenty-two practices and their sequence of implementation at Hospital Heal is highlighted in Table 16.2. The intent of sharing the sequence is not to imply that your organization should follow the same, but to show what worked for Hospital Heal's culture. These practices were initially tested in the pilot areas before being introduced across the organization. My endeavor is to provide senior executive leaders and organizational excellence practitioners with a starting point, a direction, a reference line, and an example of what a roadmap looks like based on my experiential learning, which is also supported by best-practice literature. I hope readers

Table 16.2 Patient and Family–Partnered Care Practices Supported by Their Respective Guiding Principles

IAP2	Mission	Core Concept	#	Guiding Principles	#	PFPC Practices	Sequence adopted at Hospital Heal
Inform	INSPIRE a culture of CARE Engaging hearts and minds to promote Patient and Family Partnered Care	Dignity & Respect	1	PF feedback is welcomed and acted upon to improve patient outcomes	1	PF Experience Survey	1
			2	Patients easily identify care team members	2	NOD - Name - Occupation - Duty	4
			3	All processes and practices are examined through the patient's lens	3	PFPC Orientation Package	5
			4	Patient cultural needs, wishes, and preferences are sought and respected	4	Cultural Competency Training	
Consult			5	Care team members welcome family presence	5	Supporting Family Presence	
	INVOLVE Patients and Families in their CARE Including Patients and Families in discussions and decisions in their care	Information Sharing	6	Information flow keeps PF involved in their care journey	6	Patient Profiles	10
					7	Care Team Member Profiles	12
					8	Patient White Boards	11
					9	Patient Passport - SMART Admission	
					10	Patient Passport - SMART Discharge	
					11	Health Literacy	
					12	Teach Back	
Involve					13	Shared Medical Records	
	IMPROVE Quality and Experience of CARE together Partnering with Patients and Families in service design, delivery, and evaluation	Participation	7	PF are meaningfully engaged with their care team	14	Its SAFE to Ask	6
					15	Nurse Bedside Shift Report	9
					16	Nurse Bedside hourly rounding	
					17	Shared Care Plans - Bedside Care Rounds	8
					18	Shared Care Plans (One Patient One Plan)	7
Collaborate		Collaboration	8	Care team members partner with PF in the design, delivery, and evaluation of services to improve the patient experience	19	PF as Partners in Projects	3
					20	Patient Stories	2
Empower					21	Advisory Roles	
					22	PF Shadowing	

IAP2 - International Association for Public Participation

Legend: PFPC= Patient and Family Partnered Care; PF= Patients and Family

find the roadmap useful to initiate discussions with their teams and to create their own roadmap suitable to meet their organization's needs.

Sensei Gyaan: *An organization will fail to achieve the desired results of their transformational journey without integrating the management system elements into their daily operations. To change an organizational culture and ensure that the gains of implementation are locked in and sustained, it is imperative that the following two conditions be met:*

1. *Leadership sets the behavior expectations to live the organization values and provides an environment in which those behaviors can thrive.*
2. *Employees demonstrate a conscious change of behavior in their daily work.*

Chapter 17

Develop a Communication Plan with a High Degree of Visual Management to Support Branding

> *The single biggest problem in communication is the illusion that it has taken place.*
>
> **—George Bernard Shaw**

Based on several studies conducted on nonverbal communication by Dr. Albert Mehrabian, 7% of any message is conveyed through words, 38% through certain vocal elements, and 55% through nonverbal elements (visual appeal, facial expressions, gestures, posture, etc.). Therefore, in a transformational journey it is important to strategize with all three communication methods (verbal, nonverbal, and vocal) to engage people at all levels.

As a first step, understand your target audience and plan your communication strategy to meet their need. Use a stakeholder analysis grid to plot all of your key stakeholders (Figure 17.1).

Use the template (Table 17.1) to develop your communication plan.

In their book, *Made to Stick*, Dan and Chip Heath share six principles (SUCCESs) that can be applied as a template or checklist to shape or test any idea/message for stickiness (Figure 17.2). A sticky idea/message is one that is understandable, memorable, effective, and actually changes perspectives or

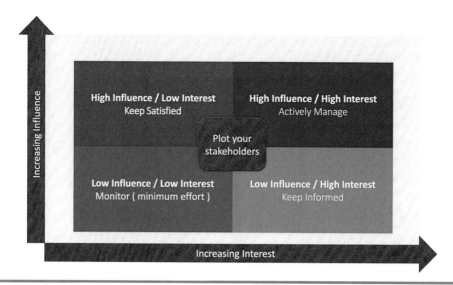

Figure 17.1 **Strategies for managing stakeholders.**

behaviors. Not all ideas are "stick-worthy," though it is possible to systematically create sticky ideas/messages. Develop a communication strategy that sticks with your target audience.

A recent survey conducted by Innovisor revealed that 3% of employees (the "key influencers") drive organizational conversations with 90% of the other employees. When incoming CEO Jack Rowe launched a turnaround journey at Aetna Inc., he kept in direct personal contact with nearly one hundred leaders in multiple levels and functions. These informal networks not only brought him up to speed on the way people thought about their

Table 17.1 **Template to Develop a Communication Plan**

Target Audience	Purpose	Message	Method of Delivery	Date of Delivery	Owner
Who am I directing my communication to?	Why are we planning this activity?	What is the core message that you are delivering to them?	How are you going to deliver the message?	When are you going to deliver this message?	Who is developing and delivering this communication activity to the audience?

SIMPLE   UNEXPECTED   CONCRETE   CREDIBLE   EMOTIONAL   STORIES

image: Heath Brothers

Figure 17.2   Dan and Chip Heath's Six Principles of Stickiness.

work and the practices they followed, but became viral spreaders of the culture he wanted to evolve.

Sensei Gyaan: *In your transformational journey, find the 3% who are most frequently identified as influential by their peers and leverage them to engage people at all levels using social networking.*

Now, let us continue to learn from the real case example of More Time to Care at Hospital Heal. Some of the strategies implemented at Hospital Heal, as a part of their multilevel communication plan to engage the frontline, managers, directors, senior team, and physicians, included the following:

■ Leaders demonstrated living the new behavior to support the excellence journey (Figure 17.3)

Figure 17.3   Leaders conduct "Go See Learn" visits at Hospital Heal.

- More Time to Care added as a standing agenda item on the monthly physician leadership meeting, weekly director meeting, weekly senior team meeting, and monthly quality committee of the board meeting
- More Time to Care Council with representation from different departments established
- Weekly meetings between the communications department and transformation office regularized
- More Time to Care branding created and incorporated as a part of all standard work templates and presentations (Figure 17.4)
- More Time to Care portal created on the intranet
- Lean overview included as part of new employee orientation
- Lean education made mandatory as part of employees' professional development
- Live skits and videos on standard work created
- Blogs posted on intranet
- More Time to Care education fair held annually to share management system elements implemented in pilot areas. The fair included booths for creating awareness on Lean tools and poster presentations to showcase the projects implemented (Figure 17.5)
- 8 × 4-foot visual whiteboards displaying department performance scorecard metrics facilitated team huddles (Figure 17.6 shows the actual board)

Figure 17.4 **Standard templates and branding.**

Figure 17.5 **Annual education fair.**

- "Traveling roadshows" conducted quarterly or as needed by the value stream coaches to answer any questions, provide quick updates, and impart education on standard work
- Individuals and teams recognized monthly during improvement project report-out events in the auditorium
- Project priority validation sessions held quarterly with directors, physicians, and senior team
- Biweekly meetings held between the transformation leader and chief of staff
- Portable "huddle boards" rolled in during physician meetings to discuss quick wins and other challenges experienced by the clinical departments

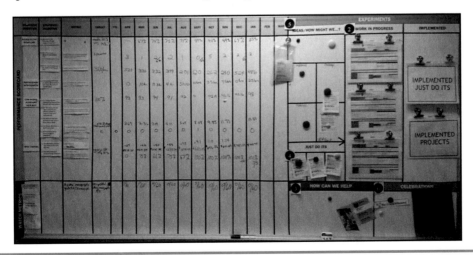

Figure 17.6 **Performance Scorecard visual board: 8 × 4-foot porcelain magnetic whiteboard.**

While all the above strategies were very effective, I would like to make a special mention of two: (1)members of the leadership team acting as role models to influence change and (2) the huddle/scorecard board. These two strategies were not time or event based. They were visible to both staff and patients at all times and therefore became instrumental in impacting behavior change across the organization.

Let me first share the innovative and highly visual layout of the performance scorecard board. While the left side of the board had the provision to display area-specific metrics and monitor performance on a monthly basis, the right side of the board allowed the team to conduct their daily/weekly huddles and see the linkage of the projects/initiatives with the metrics at all times (Figure 17.6). All eighty performance scorecard boards were installed across the hospital in areas that were accessible to patients and families. Patients were encouraged to attend huddles along with staff and learn about the work being done to positively impact their health outcomes. To promote standardization, the design of the performance scorecard board mirrored the concept of the four walls of the visual strategy room.

Before procuring the porcelain magnetic whiteboard, eighty paper versions of the scorecards, 8 × 4 feet, were professionally printed, in a standard template and tested in all areas across the hospital for its layout, content, and location for a trial period of ninety days (Figure 17.7). In addition, standard work definitions (refer to the template below) were created for interpreting the contents of the board. Education was provided to all staff for reviewing their performance scorecard/huddle board on a set frequency.

Standard Work Definitions for Performance Scorecard/Huddle Board
Performance Scorecard:
[Yellow section] Department metrics cascaded from the strategic directions and objectives that the team plans to work actively to improve during the year
Watch Metrics:
[Blue section] Metrics that the team wants to keep an eye on—no active work proposed
Strategic Direction:
As defined in the strategy document of Hospital Heal
Strategic Objective:
As defined in the strategy document of Hospital Heal

(Continued)

Standard Work Definitions for Performance Scorecard/Huddle Board
Metric:
Parameters or measures of quantitative assessment used for measurement, comparison, or tracking performance
Target:
Goal that the team decides to achieve for a metric
YTD Indicator:
Cumulative measure of actual performance of the metric from the beginning of the fiscal year to the reporting date compared to the target for the same period
The indicator is green when actual performance > target. Yellow means up to 10% deviation from the target (except for financial budget where a deviation of up to 1% is considered yellow). Red indicates > 10% deviation from the target (except for financial budget where a deviation > 1% is considered red).
Ideas/How Might We …?:
A concept/thought that a team member would like to experiment with to improve operational metrics or team culture
Just Do It's:
Projects or initiatives that can be implemented within 4 weeks. Just Do It's do not require a project charter. Teams are allowed to implement a maximum of three projects concurrently.
Experiments:
[Green section] All initiatives being undertaken to move the metrics toward its target
Work in Progress:
Projects with a defined charter that support the metrics
Ideally, no more than three projects should be worked on concurrently.
Implemented:
Results of completed projects
PICK Chart:
Tool used to help prioritize ideas by determining the work effort and impact of each idea

Possible: Low effort + Low impact
    Implement: Low effort + High impact
    Challenge: High effort + High impact
    Kibosh: High effort + Low impact

(Continued)

Standard Work Definitions for Performance Scorecard/Huddle Board			
How Can We Help?:			
[Red section] Issues requiring assistance inside/outside the department that need escalation to support			
Celebrations:			
[Blue section] Area to recognize accomplishments: projects implemented, good news, compliments, etc.			
Killer Phrases (Statements that Kill Idea Generation):			
1. A good idea, but… 2. Against policy 3. All right in theory 4. Be practical 5. Costs too much 6. Don't start anything yet 7. It needs more study	8. Not in the budget 9. Not enough time 10. Not part of my job 11. Let's survey first 12. Let's sit on it for a bit 13. Not our problem 14. The boss won't go for it	15. Too hard to administer 16. We've never done it that way 17. Who else has tried it? 18. Now you've gone too far 19. Let's form a committee 20. We tried that two years ago and it didn't work	21. If it's such a good idea, why hasn't it been suggested before? 22. The old timers won't get it 23. We've been doing it this way for a long time and it works

Figure 17.7   **Paper versions of scorecards tested in all eighty areas across the hospital.**

Many senior leaders ask why in the age of Big Data you would want to install giant whiteboards and expect people to update them manually. They fear that after some time the boards will become expensive wallpaper occupying premium wall space that no one will use. My response is that I am not against the use of technology, provided it does not take an opportunity away from teams to huddle, share problems, and leverage the strength of their team members to solve problems collectively; limit access to information to a select few; curtail transparency and open communication within and among staff, patients, and customers; and prevent staff from relating their work to organizational strategy.

In my view, use technology to extract data on metrics but do not substitute it for a visual board. It is too big a price to pay if the excellence journey fails. Instead, establish standard work, integrate the new way of working into employees' daily work, motivate and recognize staff, and invest in professional development, all of which will give the best return on your investment. You will be glad you made that investment in procuring the visual boards.

Sensei Gyaan: *The purpose of the visual management is to make the abnormal obvious. In case of daily visual management, first focus on the management (what you want to do), then on the visual (how), followed by the daily (when) (Figures 17.8 and 17.9).*

Now let's talk about the second strategy of leadership as a role model in influencing organizational change. In Chapter 3, we learned that leadership

Figure 17.8 **Leadership huddles or walk-arounds without visual controls are "social visits."**

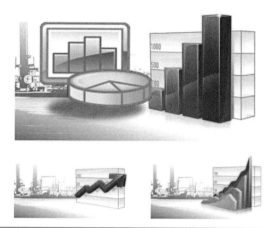

Figure 17.9 **Visual controls without leadership huddles become "wallpaper."**

commitment and systems and structures in the CAP model are pre-requisites for any change effort and they support all the other five categories of the CAP model throughout the course of the excellence journey. The two have to work hand in glove to inspire culture change in the organization. In successful companies, culture doesn't happen by accident. It occurs because leaders are modeling behaviors that lead to success.

The hospital report card, the performance scorecards, the strategy room, the Go See Learn, and the huddle boards are all examples of providing an environment, but the critical component is how leadership takes personal responsibility to be a role model for staff in demonstrating the new way of working in the organization. In his book *The Company that Solved Health Care*, John Torinus, CEO of Serigraph, says, "We do not have leader standard work and that is the biggest barrier why we can't go as fast as we want in this continuous improvement journey."

The leadership presence around the visual board is a good example of setting the tone of behavior expected from the staff and demonstrating commitment to several of the sustenance elements shared earlier, including the performance scorecard, visual management, team huddles, no-meeting zone, Go See Learn, team-based creative problem solving, coaching, leader standard work, recognition, scorecard review, and reflection. For that reason, I have highlighted the importance of having a visual huddle board in every area of the organization.

Chapter 18

Develop Processes to Celebrate Experiments and to Recognize Individuals and Teams

Creativity is inventing, experimenting, growing, taking risks, breaking rules, making mistakes, and having fun.

—Mary Lou Cook

A transformational change journeys can be exhausting; time consuming; and physically, mentally, and emotionally draining, but it does not always have to be that way. Having fun, celebrating small wins, encouraging creativity and experimentation, supporting one another during difficult times, saying thank you more often, and appreciating one another's perspective can make a huge positive impact on the organization's environment. Often ignored as trivial or time consuming, these behaviors are instrumental in the journey to organizational excellence and culture transformation.

The Institute of Healthcare Improvement (IHI) in their white paper, "IHI Framework for Improving Joy in Work" summarizes the results of their study on the impact of "joy in work" and conclude that it not only impacts individual staff engagement and satisfaction, but also patient experience, quality of care, patient safety, and organizational performance. The paper shares the nine elements of the framework for the joy in work (Figure 18.1) and

Figure 18.1 **IHI Framework for improving joy in work.**

discusses how happy, healthy productive teams and systems in an enterprise of healing contribute to creating a culture that encourages and fosters trust, improvement, and joy in work.

The authors emphasize that transformation requires "joy in work" and senior leaders are responsible for ensuring physical and psychological safety, articulating the organization's purpose, providing a clear line of sight from the work of each person to the mission of the organization, and ensuring meaning and purpose in work. Leaders ensure fair, equitable systems that embody the fundamental human needs that drive joy in work. By understanding daily work, leaders recognize the context in which colleagues work, ensure the effectiveness of systems, and identify opportunities to make improvements and celebrate outcomes.

James Quincey, CEO of Coca Cola, says the tone of culture has to be set by the top management: "You have to be clear and consistent with your people. We must not overinvest time and energy on making things perfect.

In this new world, we need to get a version 1.0 quickly, from which we learn. If something doesn't work, we stop it. And that's perfectly okay. If something is good but not perfect, we need a 2.0 fast, and then a 3.0 version. We then scale what is successful. We must be bold and fast, and we have to execute and perform. We need to have the mentality of a technology company. In order for this cultural change to work out, leaders must set an example." Mark Zuckerberg, CEO of Facebook too believes, "Done is better than perfect," meaning that being perfect is not important, but getting the job done matters.

Mistakes are the portals of discovery. Thomas A. Edison said, "I have not failed. I've just found 10,000 ways that won't work." Neuroscience researcher Alex Korb says, "Trying for the best, instead of good enough, brings too much emotional ventromedial prefrontal activity into the decision-making process. In contrast, recognizing that good enough is good enough activates more dorsolateral prefrontal areas, which helps you feel more in control." To stimulate a culture of innovation, encourage (1) diversity, (2) permission to fail, (3) experimentation, (4) learning fast and cheap, and (5) the ability to pick up weak signals. Does your organization celebrate the festival of failure? If not, start one soon.

Some of the other opportunities created to celebrate experiments and recognize individuals and teams at Hospital Heal included:

- Leadership presence during Go See Learns
- CARE awards
- Monthly project report-outs in the auditorium
- Kudos cards
- Tokens of appreciation
- Thank-you cards from the CEO

"Perfection is the enemy of good" was wholeheartedly promoted and lived at Hospital Heal. For that reason, the title on the huddle boards read "Experiments." Employees were encouraged to explore, experiment, and learn from their experiences. Also, ensuring that the huddle board had a placeholder titled "Celebrations" encouraged in-the-moment recognitions of individuals and teams (Figure 18.2). The idea was to celebrate the lessons from reflection and not just successes alone.

In their book *Gung Ho!*, the authors, Ken Blanchard and Sheldon Bowles, while describing the principle of "*The Gift of the Goose: Cheering Others On*," say, "Active or passive, congratulations must be TRUE—Timely, Responsive,

Figure 18.2 **Teams at Hospital Heal celebrating their first huddle and scorecard.**

Unconditional, Enthusiastic." In the football game analogy, the authors mention that fans don't sit mute as the ball is moved down the field, waiting for the touchdown before cheering. They lay the emphasis on cheering the progress as opposed to just the results. They say, "Measurement shared with everyone generates excitement." Senior management can infuse energy by reinforcing what is working well, and spotlighting success. Stories crystallize the effects of change and inspire confidence.

In Figure 18.3, you would note that the quadrants labeled "Process" and "Innovation and Growth" are diagonal to each other, which means if you allow innovation and growth culture to thrive in an organization, you have to be less stringent with your processes. Likewise, organizations who wish to be more competitive in the marketplace, will have to reduce time spent by people on small talk and water cooler talk, and instead use that time in implementing benchmarking strategies. The amount of diagonal tension that is acceptable depends upon the risk aptitude of your organization and the culture you want to build.

High performance organizations promote healthy tensions between teams without creating chaos in the organization. Structured chaos is better than random chaos. The provision of the huddle board is a good illustration of allowing structured chaos. Teams huddle, discuss, challenge, and celebrate one another around the goals that are meaningful to their department,

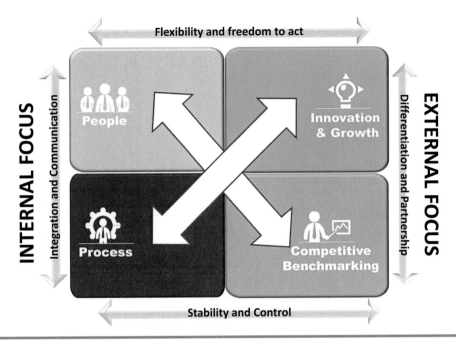

Figure 18.3   **Tensions between diagonal cultures.**

thereby creating constructive chaos, instead of everyone randomly wanting to do their own thing and creating disruptive chaos. Disruption is good when teams want to do something radical to achieve a bigger goal as a team, not as an individual. Therefore, the need for establishing a process that is repeatable and instills behavior change takes precedence over an event-based activity.

Another example from Hospital Heal, shared below, was the development of standard template (Figure 18.4) for conducting monthly report-outs for sharing improvement initiatives. All teams were provided a format, time duration, and venue to share their work with others and get recognized.

Structure sound boring, doesn't it? You may think that the report-outs would be a snore fest. However, you may be surprised to learn that the monthly report-outs were the most awaited and sought-after event. They drew staff to a full-house auditorium at least 10–15 minutes before the start to secure a good seat. The report-outs were a fun event where teams showcased not just the technical content but also their creative talent in the selection of props, theater lighting, songs, costumes, and much more (Figure 18.5). The ambience created supercharged individuals and motivated them to take personal accountability in changing their behavior toward problem solving and delivering results.

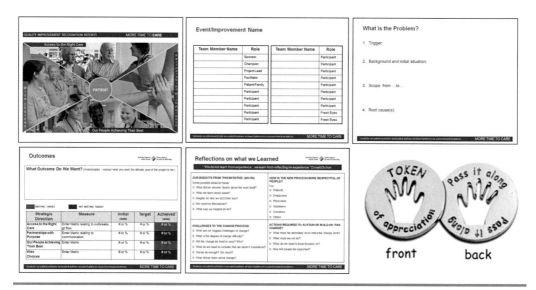

Figure 18.4 Standard template for sharing improvements undertaken during monthly report-out events.

Figure 18.5 Full house during monthly report-outs in the auditorium at Hospital Heal.

Sensei Gyaan: *Encourage the use of a pencil instead of a pen to remind leaders that continuous improvement is all about change, that very little is permanent, and what may be good today could be a thing of the past, as new information is made available.*

Chapter 19

Develop Content for Standard Work on Management System Elements and Other Educational Material to Support the Excellence Journey

The real voyage of discovery consists of not in seeking new landscapes but in having new eyes.

—Marcel Proust

Everyone understands the need for developing educational material and standard work in an excellence journey. However, what often gets missed is development of a standard work process to create standard work. It may seem like an extra step but it isn't. The standard work content developed in consultation with the staff (and physicians in the case of healthcare) has a much higher probability of acceptance by teams across the organization as compared to the one created by the centralized corporate team in isolation. Let me illustrate what a standard work process looks like, with an example from Hospital Heal (Figure 19.1).

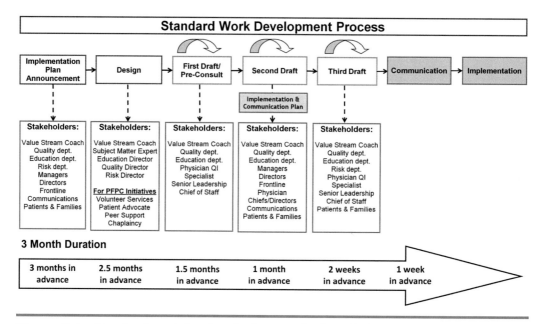

Figure 19.1 Standard work for developing standard work for all management system elements at Hospital Heal.

The core team engaged the leadership team every quarter to decide which management system element(s) would be introduced in the rolling year. Working backward from the date of launch, the development of standard work for any management system element was a three-month process. An initial announcement was made to the staff informing them on the plan to introduce a new management system element in any one or more pilot area(s), three months in advance. In consultation with the subject matter expert and the communications team, an initial draft was created. The first draft was shared with the senior leadership, which included the chief of staff, for their in-principal acceptance of the broad outline of the standard work, the language used, and what the management system was expected to achieve, six weeks in advance of the launch date. A second draft with the necessary changes was then shared with the directors, managers, frontline personnel, and other physicians for their input on the content. Changes were incorporated in the third draft and shared with the senior leadership team for their final review and feedback two weeks prior to launch. The communications team then prepared a communications package and implemented a multiplatform strategy to reach the target audience one week in advance of the launch date.

Having a standard work development process clearly articulated to everyone in the organization completely eliminated any last-minute surprises, significantly reduced resistance from the pilot areas for introducing the management system elements in their area, and allowed teams to plan their workload during the implementation period.

Likewise, while developing the standard educational material for new staff orientation, creating awareness among staff on process-improvement tools and methodologies, project management, change management, innovation, creative problem solving, coaching and facilitation, etc., it is important that the language and terminology used resonate with the culture of your organization. Hospital Heal replaced the Japanese nomenclature with easy-to-understand English terms such as CQI (continuous quality improvement) instead of Kaizen; Go See Learn instead of Gemba Genchi Genbutsu; reflection instead of Hansei; strategic planning instead of Hoshin Kanri; waste instead of Muda; horizontal deployment instead of Yokaten; and beginner, intermediate, and advanced levels instead of yellow, green, and black belt Lean Six Sigma, among others.

Several examples of standard work for management system elements created for Hospital Heal are shared in the Appendix of this book to provide leaders and practitioners with a means to manage their businesses better. Note that standard work for all management system elements and the educational material for staff at Hospital Heal were developed in-house. A special shout-out to all members of the Hospital Heal family that included frontline workers, managers, directors, and physicians, vice presidents, and the CEO, who not only contributed to the continuous iterative development process but also had the courage to lead the implementation and promote standard work for all management system elements, during the transformation period. The core team collectively spent several hundred hours in content design, which included many late-night pizza dinners. The excitement to be part of creating something from scratch cannot be expressed in words; it has to be lived. I admit, I still have fond memories of those best times that we spent together as a team. We are all very proud of the work we delivered and the lessons and standard work templates presented here in this book are our way to "pay it forward."

Sensei Gyaan: *Develop the education material in-house only if you have a seasoned expert to facilitate content development. Otherwise it is best to take outside help for initial support. Steal shamelessly from others who have gone before you. However, customize content and language to suit your organization's culture.*

Chapter 20

Build the Problem-Solving Muscle of the Organization

Education is the most powerful weapon which you can use to change the world.

—Nelson Mandela

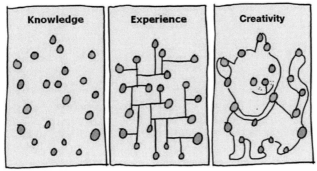

Training for professional skill and leadership development is by far the most important element in engaging employees while they experience change during an organization's transformation journey. In today's business environment, organizations across industries have realized the importance of training employees in creative and innovative approaches to problem solving as important skills for success. Some of the organizations are not just solving problems creatively, but also defining, measuring, and analyzing problems innovatively. To give an example, a hospital measured lead time for their emergency department admission process in "5D's": door (arrive in ED) to doctor to decision to done to depart (admit to unit).

Hospital Heal trained their staff in creative and innovative approach to problem solving using the Simplexity Thinking System, whose developer, Min Basadur, says, "Developing people in creative problem solving makes people better at finding problems. That may sound odd until you consider that innovation requires new solutions—and new solutions require anticipating problems, changes, trends and opportunities." "Every act of creation is first an act of destruction," said Pablo Picasso.

Creating a plan with a five-year time horizon provides a big-picture view to the organization in terms of who would be trained, what they would be trained in, and how much budget would be required. The plan allows leaders to do workforce planning for scheduling and backfilling key positions, and getting their commitment on resource availability for training and development. The number of people and their frequency of training over the five-year period, however, depends upon what objective the organization wants to achieve in the end. Table 20.1 shows an example of a training plan for engaging employees in the transformational journey undertaken at Hospital Heal.

Table 20.1 Business Excellence Training Plan for Engaging Employees at Hospital Heal

		All percentages (%) are cummulative and on an employee base of 2400					
		YEAR 0	YEAR 1	YEAR 2	YEAR 3	YEAR 4	YEAR 5
Core Team and Value Stream Coach	Best Practice Site Visit(s)	100%	100%	100%	100%	100%	100%
	Lean Thinking - Intermediate	100%	100%	100%	100%	100%	100%
	Lean Management	100%	100%	100%	100%	100%	100%
All employees and physicians but excluding Senior Leadership Team (SLT)	Lean Awareness		40%	100%	100%	100%	100%
	Lean Thinking - Beginners		5%	15%	30%	50%	75%
	Lean Thinking - Intermediate		1%	2.5%	5%	8%	10%
All employees excluding physicans and SLT	Lean Thinking - Advanced			0.20%	0.40%	0.60%	0.75%
Managers, Directors, Medical Chiefs	Best Practice Site Visit(s)	20%	40%	100%	100%	100%	100%
	Lean Management		40%	100%	100%	100%	100%
SLT including Chief of Staff	Best Practice Site Visit(s)	100%	100%	100%	100%	100%	100%
	Lean Awareness	100%	100%	100%	100%	100%	100%
	Lean Thinking - Beginners		25%	50%	100%	100%	100%
	Lean Thinking - Intermediate		25%	50%	75%	100%	100%
	Lean Management		75%	100%	100%	100%	100%
Board members	Best Practice Site Visit(s)	20%	40%	100%	100%	100%	100%
	Lean Awareness		100%	100%	100%	100%	100%
	Lean Thinking - Beginners			25%	50%	75%	100%

In Table 20.1, Year 0 represents the year dedicated to establishing foundational elements for the excellence journey, part of which included site visits to other best-practice hospitals, as well as grooming the core team and the value stream coaches (Figures 20.1 and 20.2).

A word of caution for organizations who define success by only measuring "number of employees trained" in a particular period: in my experience, the number of employees trained, by itself, is a very weak metric because it fails to inform the impact on organizational performance. Therefore, it is best to support the training metric with other measures such as "% staff trained who led at least one project," "number of ideas generated/implemented," "amount of time/dollars saved," or "percent increase in time spent in value-added activities," etc., each of which can be measured at an individual or team level.

As mentioned in Chapter 6, the central core team at Hospital Heal was comprised of individuals that had expertise in the knowledge areas listed in the Business Excellence Model (Figure 6.3). The value stream coaches,

Figure 20.1   Core team and value stream coaches trained at Hospital Heal.

Figure 20.2   Core team and value stream coaches leading a session at Hospital Heal.

on the other hand, were full-time dedicated resources from frontline operations that were seconded for a period of thirty months to undergo training with the core team for an initial period of six months and then facilitate change in the operational areas of clinical, mental health, and corporate, for the remaining period of twenty-four months. The intent was that upon completion of their tenure, the individuals would assume leadership roles in the organization and new value stream coaches would replace them.

The rigorous in-house training provided to the core team and value stream coaches included self-study, in-class sessions, practical simulations, and hands-on real applications. (Note that ISO 18404:2015 has now come up with uniform standards to certify both organizations and individuals in either Six Sigma, Lean, or both.)

Among many definitions of Lean, the one below resonates with me the most.

- **Lean:** A *mindset* of continuous improvement. It's a system that empowers people at all levels to remove waste and maximize what is of value to the customer. In the healthcare setting, the customer is the patient.

Don Drury, former VP of Merrill Lynch, defines quality and business quality as:

- **Quality:** The realization of value entitlement
- **Business Quality:** A state in which the customer and provider realize the mutual gratifying exchange of value

Learning through Visuals: Figures 20.3 through 20.26 and Tables 20.2 through 20.12 are select examples, worth sharing, of education content from

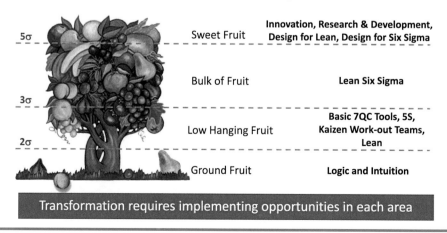

Figure 20.3   **Alternate approaches to problem solving.**

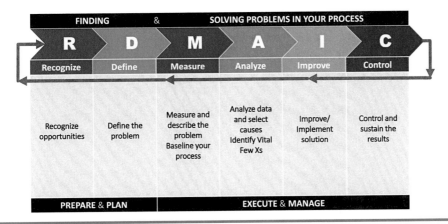

Figure 20.4 Six Sigma approach to problem solving.

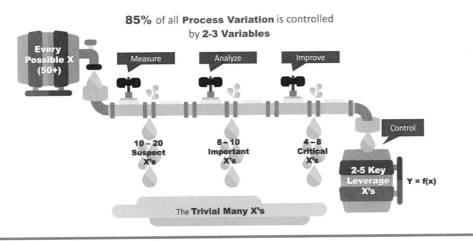

Figure 20.5 Six Sigma differentiates "vital few" from "trivial many" variables.

Figure 20.6 The five principles of Lean.

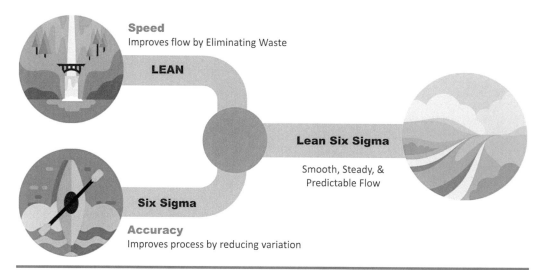

Figure 20.7   **The strength of Lean Six Sigma combined.**

Figure 20.8   **Seeing things differently.**

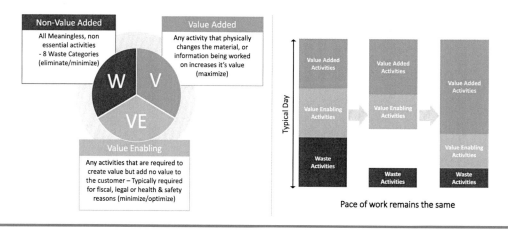

Figure 20.9   **Classifying activities using the Lean lens.**

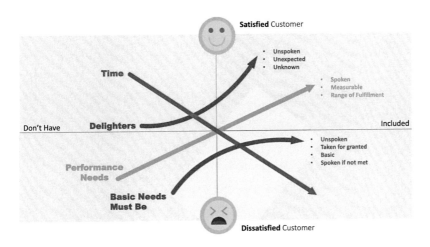

Figure 20.10   Kano model for understanding the voice of the customer.

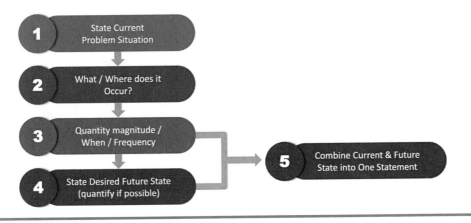

Figure 20.11   Steps for creating a problem statement.

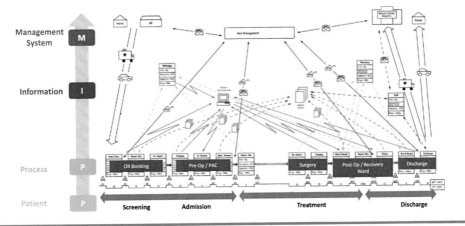

Figure 20.12   Creating a value stream map using the PPIM approach.

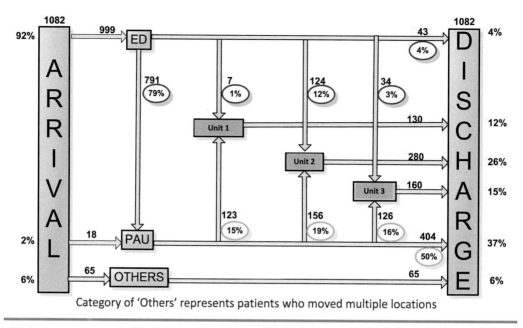

Figure 20.13 **Example of a demand map of patient flow through the ED at a hospital.**

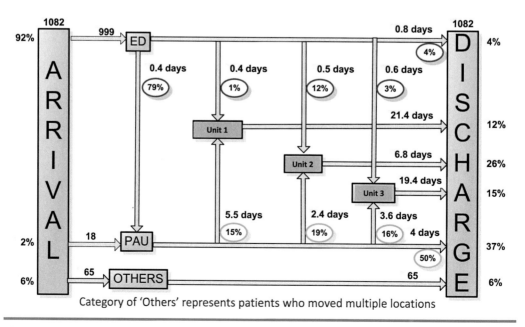

Figure 20.14 **Example of a length-of-stay (LOS) map of patients in their journey.**

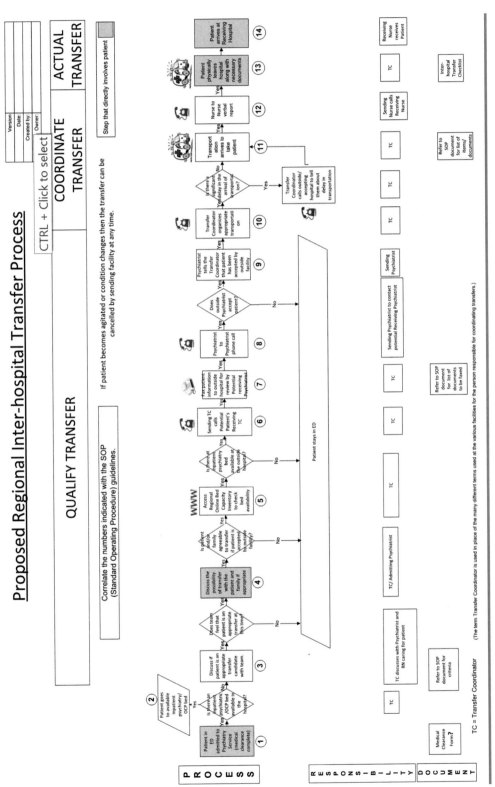

Figure 20.15 Illustration of a standard operating process.

PROBLEM: Washington Monument was deteriorating

Why is the monument deteriorating?
Use of harsh chemicals to wash the building

Why do they use harsh chemicals?
To clean bird poop

Why so many birds?
They eat spiders and there are a lot of spiders at the monument

Why so many spiders?
They eat midges (insects)and there are a lot of midges at the monument

Why so many midges?
They are attracted to light at dusk

SOLUTION: Turn on the lights at a later time

Figure 20.16   **Example of a 5 WHY analysis to understand the root cause.**

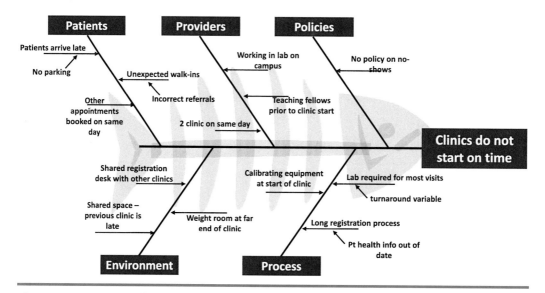

Figure 20.17   **Example of a fish bone analysis to understand cause and effect.**

Lean Thinking that I developed over the years, collected from conferences I attended, or stole shamelessly from other best-practice organizations that I visited (remember, do not reinvent the wheel).

Sensei Gyaan: *Switch to in-the-moment training and coaching as compared to full-day classroom training sessions. For in-class training, it is*

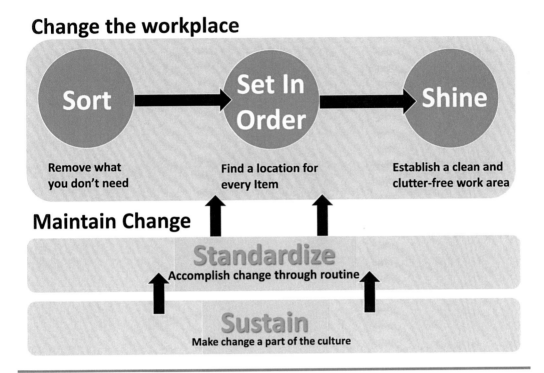

Figure 20.18 Creating an environment that has a place for everything and everything in its place.

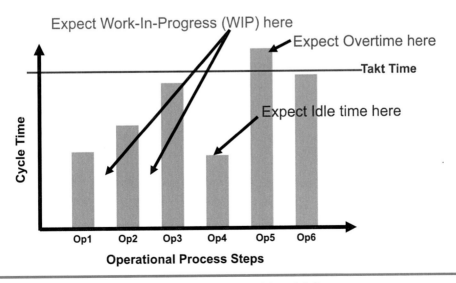

Figure 20.19 Example of an unbalanced line and its pitfalls.

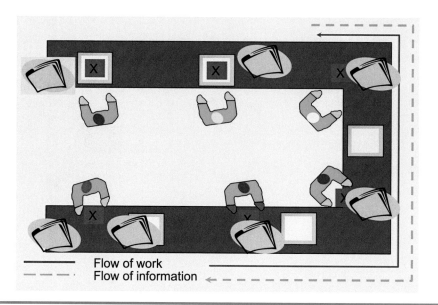

Figure 20.20   Cell design to promote single piece flow.

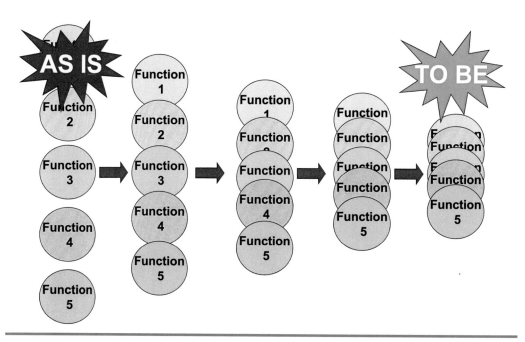

Figure 20.21   Cross train to build capacity and improve workflow.

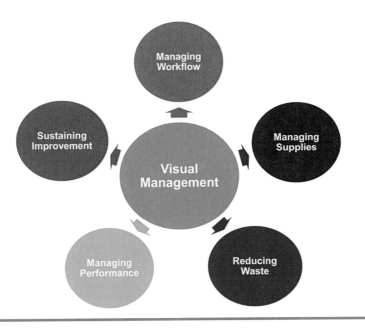

Figure 20.22   Application of visual management.

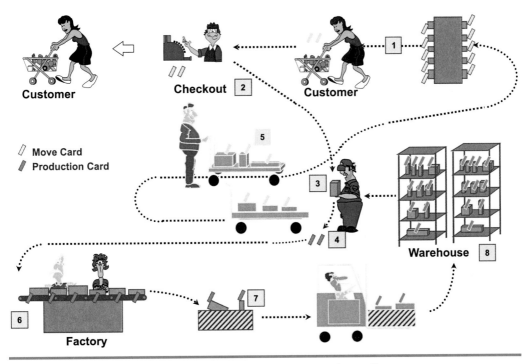

Figure 20.23   Kanban and supermarket tools support the pull system.

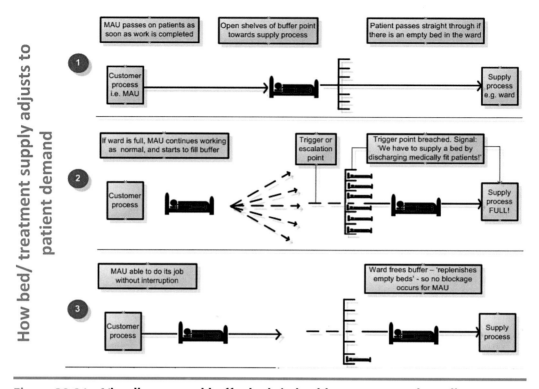

Figure 20.24 **Visually managed buffer beds in healthcare support the pull system.** (From Baker, M., I. Taylor, and A. Mitchell. How to improve patient care while saving everyone's time and hospitals' resources. *Making Hospitals Work*. Lean Enterprise Academy Limited, May 2009, p.168.)

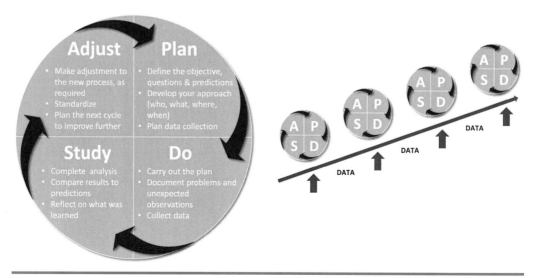

Figure 20.25 **PDSA scientific thinking: continuous-improvement cycle.**

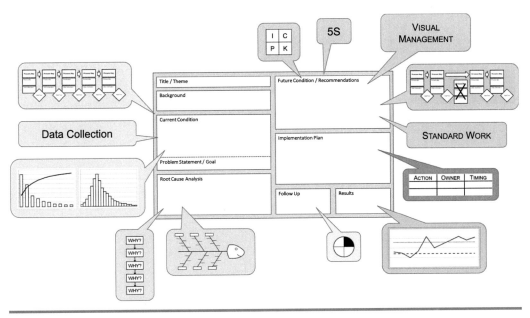

Figure 20.26 Summing up Lean Six Sigma tools in an A3 thinking template.

Table 20.2 Six Sigma's Breakthrough Equation: Output (Y) Is a Function of Input Variables (X's)

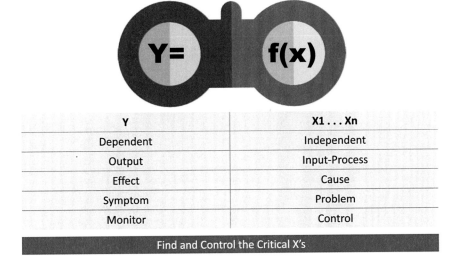

Y	X1 ... Xn
Dependent	Independent
Output	Input-Process
Effect	Cause
Symptom	Problem
Monitor	Control
Find and Control the Critical X's	

Table 20.3   Six Sigma Roadmap to Process Improvement

Phases	R Recognize	D Define	M Measure	A Analyze	I Improve	C Control
Activities	Differentiate between Value and Waste	Define current situation	Quantify the problem	Analyze potential causes	Identify potential solutions	Address human factor
	Identify opportunities and establish linkage to Strategy	Define desired situation	Identify potential causes	Select root cause(s)	Select-implement most promising	Implement control means
Deliverables	Prioritized list of opportunities	Problem Definition and Project Charter	Baseline of the problem and List of causes	Quantified causes and Root cause(s) selected	Implemented solution and Results vs Goals	A shared solution & A sustained solution

Table 20.4   Impact of Lean Application in Healthcare

Impact of Lean application in Healthcare (Industry Averages)	
Direct Labor / Productivity Improvement	45 – 75 %
Cost Savings	25 – 55 %
Space Reduced	35 – 50 %
Inventory Reduced	60 – 90 %
Rework time reduced (redundant)	50 – 90 %
Delivery Improvement	60 – 90 %

Source: Virginia Mason Medical Center

Summarized results, subsequent to a **5 year evaluation** from numerous companies. Companies ranged from **1 – 7 years** in Lean Principles application execution.

Table 20.5   Eight Types of Waste Explained Using the Acronym "DOWNTIME"

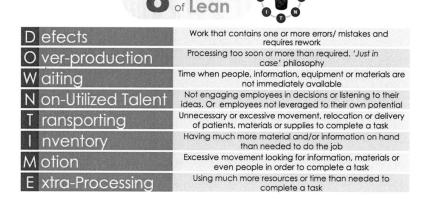

Defects	Work that contains one or more errors/ mistakes and requires rework
Over-production	Processing too soon or more than required. '*Just in case*' philosophy
Waiting	Time when people, information, equipment or materials are not immediately available
Non-Utilized Talent	Not engaging employees in decisions or listening to their ideas. Or employees not leveraged to their own potential
Transporting	Unnecessary or excessive movement, relocation or delivery of patients, materials or supplies to complete a task
Inventory	Having much more material and/or information on hand than needed to do the job
Motion	Excessive movement looking for information, materials or even people in order to complete a task
Extra-Processing	Using much more resources or time than needed to complete a task

Table 20.6   **Project Charter Template**

Performance Improvement Project Charter

PROJECT TITLE/DEPARTMENT:						
ESTIMATED PROJECT DURATION:		DATE		VERSION:		Minor change from original = 1 to 1.1 / Major change from original = 1 to 2

PROBLEM STATEMENT:

Decode the problem: Craft a simple clear statement that articulates: what? Where? How much? Since when? How do you know (Quantified (#, $, Time, %)?
Why is it important? Are their risk implications if we do nothing?
How do you know the work you will do will have an impact?
Use Objective measurable data.
Obtain data to suport that the problem exists. THINK how it links to business: Strategic Plan, Scorecard, Cost savings, Risk implecations, relationships to other projects if applicable

SCOPE: *the beginning and end points of the process for which you will be working within*

From:	To:	In: scope	Out: Of Scope
First process step- start point	Last Process step - end point	what is considered within the scope of this process? May be job classification, specific depts, locations, patient types...	what is considered outside of the scope of this project? What is excluded?

GOALS/OUTCOME:
Customer benefit

DELIVERABLES:	MEASUREMENT		
	METRIC	BASELINE	TARGET
1. Charter			
2. Current State Process: Process Flow Map, SIPOC & VSM			
3. Issues Log			
4. Prioritize opportunities (PICK chart)			
5. Future State process			
6. Standard Operating Procedure			
7. Education to stakeholders			
8. Test Pilot Standard work			
9. Metrics Evaluation at 3, 6, & 9 months post implementation (Standard Work Observation)			
10. Standardize and Go Live			

TEAM MEMBERS:	TEAM RESOURCE ALLOCATION DETAILS: (HRS/WK, ETC)		
Work directly with the process being improved			
PROJECT RESOURCES:	**STAKEHOLDERS:**		
PROJECT SPONSOR(S):			
PROJECT CHAMPION:	BUDGET:		
PROJECT LEAD:	INCLUDED IN PROJECT:	External Partner Voice — Yes ☐ No ☐ (Explain)	
		Patient Family Voice — Yes ☐ No ☐ (Explain)	
FACILITATOR:		Lit/Best Practice Review — Yes ☐ No ☐ (Explain)	
PROJECT SIGN OFF (SPONSOR):	Comments, if any:		

Table 20.7   **Example of Creating a Problem Statement for Readmission of Patients**

Question	Answer
State the current problem situation	"patients discharged are readmitted"
What/Where does it occur?	"patients from Unit XYZ, readmitted through ER"
Quantify the magnitude/ when/ frequency of problem	"During 2016, an average of 15% patients readmitted within 14 days"
State what the Future State would look like	"desired state is regional standard of 5%"
Combine current & Future State into one problem statement	"An average of 15% of patients discharged from the XYZ unit in the year 2016 are readmitted to the ER within 14 days which is 10% more than the regional standard of 5%"

Table 20.8 Identifying Stakeholders Using SIPOC

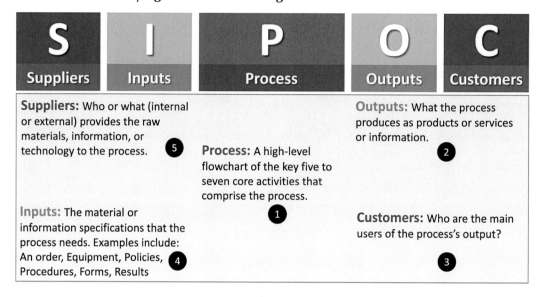

S	I	P	O	C
Suppliers	Inputs	Process	Outputs	Customers

Suppliers: Who or what (internal or external) provides the raw materials, information, or technology to the process. **(5)**

Inputs: The material or information specifications that the process needs. Examples include: An order, Equipment, Policies, Procedures, Forms, Results **(4)**

Process: A high-level flowchart of the key five to seven core activities that comprise the process. **(1)**

Outputs: What the process produces as products or services or information. **(2)**

Customers: Who are the main users of the process's output? **(3)**

Table 20.9 Creative Use of SIPOC Tool for Understanding the Big Picture

Intake Process for Geriatric Psychiatry Outreach Team (GPOT)

Where does the client come from /referred from? (Supplier)	What is the Client Need? (Input)	What is the intake process? (Process)	Where is the client referred to? (Output)	What is the Client category? (Customer)

Referral Sources:
57% Physician
19% AOA Case Manager
8% Facilities
7% MH Team
4% Central Intake
4% Family
1% Home Care
1% OPT
1% STAT
3% Other
	Reason for Referral:
	33% Assessment of Depressive Disorder
	19% Evaluation for Cognitive Impairment
	11% Neuropsych Testing
	4% Group only/Changeways
	4% Competency Assessment
	4% Agitation
	3% Paranoia/psychosis
	3% Follow-up
	2% Anxiety
	2% Consultation Only
	1% Aggression
	14% Other
	10% Urgent (Varies)
			Deceased
			Completed (No longer need GPOT)
			Mental Health Team
			Back to GP
				Average Age = 80 years
				14 patients < 65 yrs, 7 patients >95 yrs
				
				68% Female
				32% Male
				
				Axis 1 Diagnosis on Admission:
				Dementia: 39.4%
				  Alzheimer's 13%
				  Mixed 13%
				  Vascular 8%
				  Frontal Lobe 2%
				  Other 2%
				  Alcohol 1.4%
				
				Mood: 23%
				  Major Depressive Episode 13%
				  MDE-Recurrent 8%
				  Bipolar Disorder 2%
				
				Other: 37.2%
				  Cognitive Impairment NYD 8%
				  All others 8%
				  Physical Factors Affecting Psychiatric Condition 4%
				  Generalized Anxiety Disorder 3%
				  None 3%
				  Other V-Codes 3%
				  Schizophrenia - Paranoid Type 2%
				  Delusional Disorder 2%
				  Mild Cognitive Impairment 1.4%
				  Substance Related Disorder 1.4%
				  PTSD 1.4%

Timelines: Referral		24 days from referral to seen (average) (skewed by Neuropsych)	Seen	

Table 20.10   **Data Collection Methods**

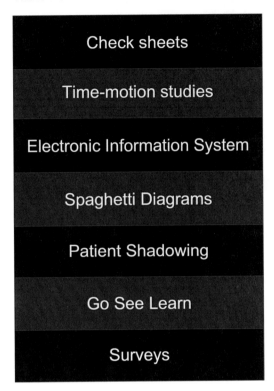

Check sheets

Time-motion studies

Electronic Information System

Spaghetti Diagrams

Patient Shadowing

Go See Learn

Surveys

Table 20.11   **Collaboration Request Template Used as a Service Level Agreement (SLA)**

Request From: *Department 1*		Request To: *Department 2*	
#	**Collaboration Request** *Dept. 1*	**Sign** *Dept. 2*	**Remarks, if parked** *Dept. 2*
1			
2			
3			
4			
5			

Table 20.12 Activities in a Rapid Improvement Event (REI)

Preparation (2 – 6 weeks)	Improvement Event (3 – 5 days)	Follow-up (30, 60, 90 days)
• Meet with sponsor • Select Team Members & Identify Stakeholders • Define the problem • Collect relevant data • Develop Charter • Communicate details • Finalize event logistics	• Review current condition • Complete root cause analysis • Brainstorm solutions and prioritize improvements • Test pilot, evaluate, and standardize changes • Present results • Communicate changes • Develop and provide appropriate training	• Follow-up on "To Do's" • Conduct follow-up meetings • Execute sustainability plan • Complete performance audit(s) • Create event report • Celebrate and communicate the results more broadly

recommended to have a maximum mix of 40% theory and balance as a practical application of the learning. Offer training only to individuals who have a real problem to solve. Do not entertain employees who want to attend training to get certified in Lean Six Sigma, or who claim to learn something new by attending. Set clear expectations with those who receive the training that, as a part of their graduation, they will be required to see one, do one, and teach one.

Chapter 21

Build a Knowledge Management System

It doesn't make sense to hire smart people and then tell them what to do; we hire smart people so they can tell us what to do.

—Steve Jobs

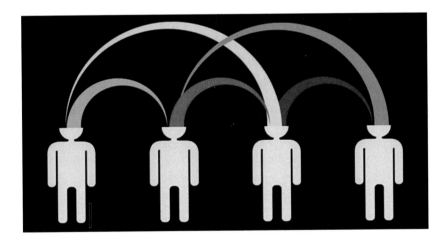

Business Dictionary.com defines knowledge management as strategies and processes designed to identify, capture, structure, value, leverage, and share an organization's intellectual assets to enhance its performance and competitiveness. John Girard & JoAnn Girard describe knowledge management as the creation, transfer, and exchange of organizational knowledge to achieve a (competitive) advantage.

Knowledge can be articulated explicitly or manifested implicitly. The main difference lies in how knowledge is shared. Explicit knowledge is clear and spoken and it can be summarized. It is therefore easier to communicate and share. Implicit knowledge, on the other hand, is rather intuitive, intangible, tacit, less teachable, less observable, unspoken, and more complex. It is more difficult to detach from the person who created it or the context in which it is embedded, which makes it hard to distinguish. The aim of knowledge management is to maximize organizational and individual knowledge by extracting implicit knowledge and translating it into explicit knowledge, which can then be interpreted, stored, retrieved, shared, and disseminated. Knowledge carried by an individual only realizes its commercial potential when it is replicated by an organization and becomes organizational knowledge.

Many organizations invest in decision support systems, database management systems, groupware, and document management systems to cater to two primary needs: (1) meet mandatory reporting requirement and (2) run day-to-day operations. Very few organizations actually invest in developing systems to leverage knowledge that individuals and teams acquire or create over the period of their work tenure, for future use or for horizontal deployment in similar applications in others areas/sites of the same organization. The result is that when the individual leaves the organization, the information leaves with him/her, leaving the organization high and dry. A recent survey confirmed that the lost knowledge of a departing employee, given the enormous number of baby boomers that will be changing jobs or retiring in the next few years, causes a productivity cost of 85% of their base salary due to their replacement's mistakes, lost knowledge, and lost skill. The 2017 National Healthcare Retention and RN Staffing Report highlighted that every 1% increase in registered nursing staff turnover costs a hospital an average of $410,500 annually. Under Lean, this is considered a waste of non-utilized talent.

According to Stankosky, knowledge management consists of four elements: organization, leadership, learning, and technology (Figure 21.1).

- **Organization:** Affects the operational parts of the knowledge resources such as organizational structures, traceability, techniques for the transmission of knowledge, and the optimized use of the company's knowledge resources.

Figure 21.1   Stankosky's elements of knowledge management.

- **Leadership:** Affects the strategic processes such as values, goals, knowledge needs, sources of knowledge, priorities, and allocation of integrated leadership and systems thinking.
- **Learning:** Affects mainly the social dimension of how individuals and communities of practice collaborate and share knowledge. The focus is on finding the attributes that create a learning organization.
- **Technology:** Focuses on groupware, collaboration tools, product mining, and various technical solutions that support knowledge management processes and strategies.

Peter Drucker said that the knowledge worker who worked primarily with his mind and not his hands would become increasingly productive in the modern workforce. He speculated that firms that first discovered how best to utilize this experienced talent in a new type of relationship would acquire a significant competitive advantage.

Martin Skogmalm, in his study on "Knowledge Management in a Lean Organization," cites that the implementation of knowledge management fails mainly due to two reasons: culture and leadership. He says that in order to stimulate knowledge management and knowledge sharing, an open organizational culture is needed, where the emphasis is on trust and building relationships, and the culture is supported through engaged leadership. Peter Senge, author of *The Fifth Discipline*, emphasizes that experienced colleagues and managers have a huge responsibility to create a culture where lessons learned are a natural part of everyday life. His book highlights the five disciplines that distinguish learning organizations from more traditional organizations: systems thinking, personal mastery, mental models, building shared vision, and team learning. In a learning organization, he says, leaders

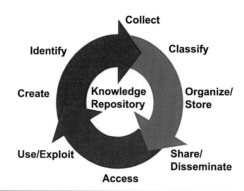

Figure 21.2 Knowledge management cycle.

are designers, stewards, and teachers. They build organizations in which people continually expand their capabilities to understand complexity and clarify vision and people are responsible for learning.

Figure 21.2 depicts the areas of opportunity during different stages of the knowledge management cycle for building a knowledge repository.

The knowledge gained during any stage of a process improvement project or initiative is a good candidate for becoming part of a central repository. For example, data collected through patient shadowing, time and motion

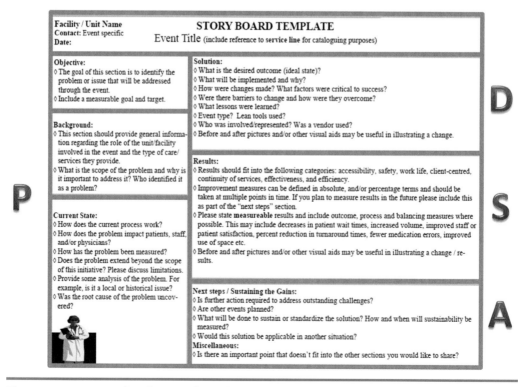

Figure 21.3 Example of a storyboard template.

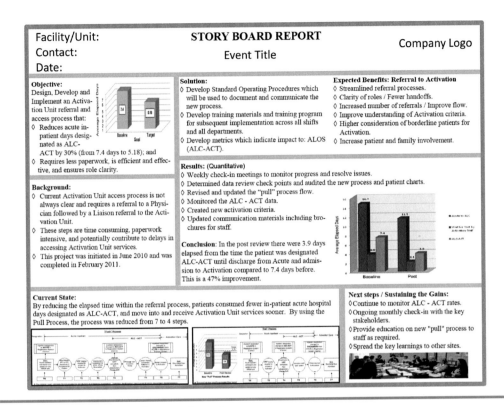

Figure 21.4   **Example of a storyboard report.**

studies, and process observations, or any analysis or simulation conducted using the data, should be retrievable on demand by anyone in the organization who needs it. While many organizations use project management solutions, business intelligence tools, learning management systems, and other technological tools to support their knowledge management, they also encourage paper-based methods such as Lean A3 to make it convenient for people at any level in the organization.

Hospital Heal procured a business intelligence tool to capture most metrics from department performance scorecards and the organizational report card. The hospital had an LMS system to maintain an inventory of training for all employees and project management software to support all continuous improvement and organization-wide projects. Examples of a storyboard template (Figure 21.3) and a completed storyboard report (Figure 21.4) based on Lean A3 thinking, which individuals and teams used at Hospital Heal for building a knowledge repository, are shared here.

Sensei Gyaan: *Use technology only after you have tested the process on paper. Remember, "Creativity before Capital."*

MONITOR PROGRESS E

Chapter 22

Define the Role of the Performance Management Team to Support the Excellence Journey

---

Think differently for different results. If we don't change direction, we will end up where we are going.

—Irwin Corey

Performance management is defined as a set of management processes, supported by information technology (IT), that enable organizations to define and execute their strategy; to measure, analyze, and monitor performance; and to align people and culture in order to inform strategic decision-making and learning.

Performance management, until lately, had been narrowly associated with people management (performance appraisals) or performance monitoring (collecting and reporting of performance indicators). More recently, the role has started to evolve toward enterprise performance management.

Enterprise Performance Management is the framework that aligns and integrates performance management with other key business processes such as financial planning, consolidation and budgeting, project and program management, people performance, reward and recognition, performance reporting, dashboards and scorecards, risk management, and business intelligence and

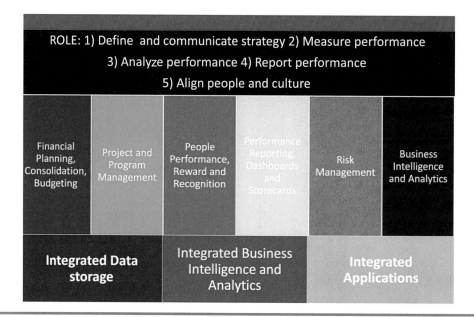

ROLE: 1) Define and communicate strategy 2) Measure performance
3) Analyze performance 4) Report performance
5) Align people and culture

| Financial Planning, Consolidation, Budgeting | Project and Program Management | People Performance, Reward and Recognition | Performance Reporting, Dashboards and Scorecards | Risk Management | Business Intelligence and Analytics |

| Integrated Data storage | Integrated Business Intelligence and Analytics | Integrated Applications |

Figure 22.1   **Components of enterprise performance management.**

analytics. These tasks are carried out with the help of technology that brings the data together in one database; provides integrated analytics and business intelligence capabilities; and integrates applications to improve the management, strategy execution, and decision-making in organizations. J. Gretzitz model on enterprise management system is one such model (Figure 22.1).

A study conducted by Development Dimensions International (DDI), found that performance management systems influence "financial performance, productivity, product or service quality, customer satisfaction, and employee job satisfaction." In addition, 79% of the CEOs surveyed said that the performance management systems implemented in their organizations drive the "cultural strategies that maximize human assets."

As per the 2017 Global survey results of PEX Network, 55% of survey respondents said they are looking to invest in strategic management solutions over the next 12 months to drive their operational excellence projects; 44% of respondents are planning on investing in data analytics and business intelligence solutions; and 40% in process modeling tools. This is expected to significantly enhance the overall domain of performance management. Emerging technologies such as artificial intelligence (AI) and robotic process automation (RPA) are predicted to change the future of how organizations will operate. The challenge however, will be to create a right balance between technology-enabled automation and domain expertise that human beings are uniquely able to bring.

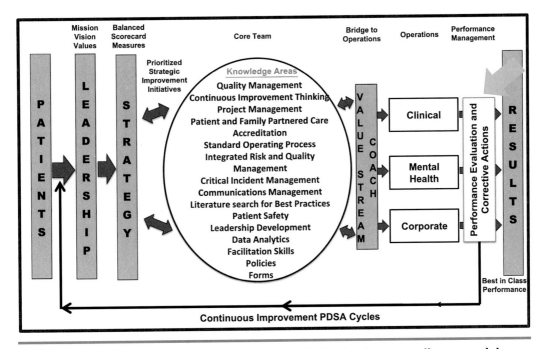

Figure 22.2 Role of performance management in the business excellence model at Hospital Heal.

In Chapter 6, I shared an example of the business excellence model implemented at Hospital Heal (Figure 22.2), where I highlighted how the performance management team supported More Time to Care in evaluating the performance of projects, initiatives, and organizational change.

Dedicated resources from performance management helped to define the metrics associated with quality improvement projects and their respective scorecards, establish the formula and baseline, and analyze and provide data to the teams across the organization to update their performance scorecards. A strategic investment made in procuring a customized business intelligence tool saved several hundred hours of manual data collection on process and outcome measures and increased the efficiency of internal and external reporting. This continuous feedback and analysis allowed teams to take timely corrective actions to address gaps and improve patient outcomes.

Sensei Gyaan: *Leverage technology to integrate and align resources, systems, and employees to the organization's strategic objectives and priorities for achieving organizational excellence. Encourage face-to-face communication and use of visual management to improve information flow and to break down work silos between departments and individuals.*

Chapter 23

Develop a Standard Tollgate Process to Evaluate the Progress of Improvement Projects

Our job is to give the client, on time and on cost, not what he wants, but what he never dreamed he wanted; and when he gets it, he recognizes it as something he wanted all the time.

—Dewys Lasdon

In Chapters 13 and 14, we learned how to categorize small, medium, and large projects and how to prioritize projects based on filters. In this chapter, I will share how to evaluate the progress of these improvement projects using a standard tollgate process.

In their article, "Using tollgate to manage your projects in action," E.Y. Romania define a tollgate as a checkpoint in a project where progress is reviewed to decide the completion stage of the activities and their objective achievements. This checkpoint serves to determine if the project can proceed to the next tollgate, also referred as a "go/no go" decision point. Only when the person leading the project confirms that the team has successfully completed the previous phase may they pass the tollgate and move to the next phase. The benefits of having a tollgate or a phase gate approach are that it helps in managing risk, facilitates

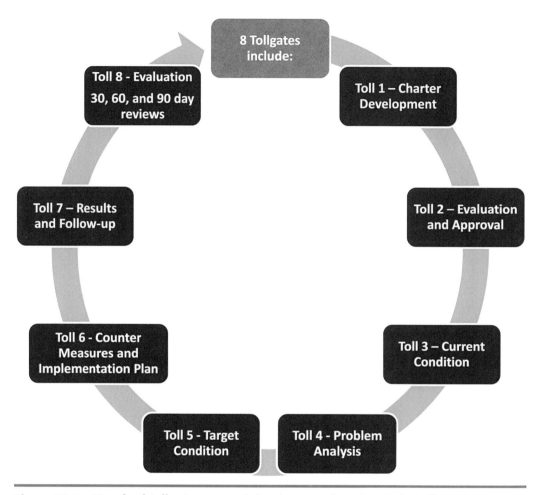

Figure 23.1   **Standard tollgate approach implemented at Hospital Heal.**

better planning, improves project management, enables informed decision-making at the steering committee level, empowers project governance, and ensures that senior-level stakeholders are engaged in the
project plan.

An important aspect is to determine where the tollgates should be
positioned in the project plan, and what activities and criteria should be
included at each tollgate. In terms of positioning, tollgates can be assigned
either by project phases or on the basis of key project milestones. The
criteria defined for each tollgate should enable an objective review of the
project's progress and to decide if the project can continue. It is essential
that the criteria defined are measurable. Consider using key phases and
completion of key milestones as central criteria. Include specific aspects

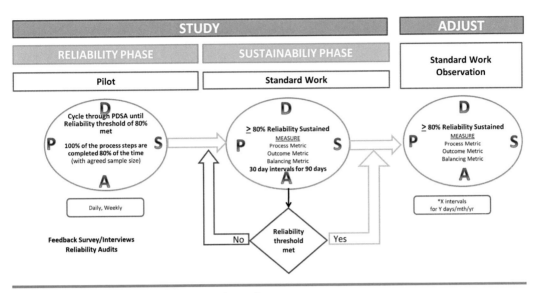

Figure 23.2 **Tollgate 8, the evaluation phase.**

of change management activities at each tollgate spread across the entire life cycle of the project.

Figure 23.1 shows an example of an eight-step standard tollgate approach developed and implemented at Hospital Heal. The project passes through different stages of Tollgates 1 through 7 before entering Tollgate 8, which is the evaluation phase. During this stage the new process is tested for its reliability before it can be moved to the sustainability phase and then to the final development of the standard work for the new process. Organizations need to define their criteria for reliability and the period of sustainability before accepting the new process. The threshold for reliability of the process in the pilot phase was ≥80% at Hospital Heal, during which time it was tested for 90 days to confirm its reliability and subsequently, a standard work observation (audit) process was established to ensure its sustainability (Figure 23.2).

Table 23.1 details the activities associated with each of the eight stages of the tollgate review process shown in Figure 23.1. These activities act as a checklist for all members of a project team and provide uniformity of the approach across different teams in an organization. If an activity is not applicable for a project, the team agrees and marks the activity as a cross in the checkbox.

Table 23.1 Activities During Each Stage of the Tollgate Review Process

TASKS

TOLL GATE REVIEW 1: VP Approves Exploratory Phase

Charter Development – Issue/Background (Exploratory Phase):
- Identify Improvement Opportunity
- Develop Problem & Objective Statements
- Identify Risks
- Identify Stakeholders/SIPOC/Analysis/VOC
- Voice of the Customer (VOC) – Patient/Family
- Collect Data
- Determine Project Scope, Deliverables, Timeframe
- Preliminary Search – Lessons Learned', Literature Review on Best Practice
- Agree on Targets/Goals
- Finalize Performance Metrics/Baselines
- Agree on Project Roles & Responsibilities
- Determine % Time commitment of Resources
- Draft Project Charter

TOLL GATE REVIEW 2: VP Approval of Charter (Exploration). Project Management Working Group Update or Evaluation & Recommendation to SLT Steering Committee (if applicable)

Current Condition:
- Communicate project commencement to stakeholders.
- Identify any Change Mgt. Requirements
- Observe process
- Develop Process Map (or Current State Value Stream Map if applicable)
- Observe process and validate data
- Collect Data & Create Demand Map (if applicable)
- e.g. spaghetti diagrams, cycle times etc.
- Create List of Opportunities for improvement in the Process (Issues Log)

Problem Analysis:
- Literature Search / Benchmarking
- Using Issues Log, create Cause and Effect Diagrams & Identify Bottlenecks e.g. 5 whys, Fishbone
- Pareto issues to determine main issues
- Select 2-4 top issues

Target Condition:
- Generate ideas on solutions for top issues
- Pick Chart Solutions
- Develop Future State Map

TOLL GATE REVIEW 3: Future State to VP (or designate) for approval

Counter Measures and Implementation Plan:
- Determine Continuous Improvement Initiatives
- Prioritize Improvement Opportunities
- Charter Initiatives
- Create action plan for initiatives
- Communicate to Stakeholders & Create/Implement Change Mgt Plan
- Initiative(s) submission to Continuous Improvement Team

TOLL GATE REVIEW 4: Project Management Working Group Evaluation & Recommendation to SLT Steering Committee

TOLL GATE REVIEW 5: VP Approval of Charter (Initiative)

30 day Results and Follow-up:
- Education
- Implement Initiative/pilot
- Confirm new process steps with stakeholders
- Create sustainability plan for trials
- Collect, analyse and evaluate data
- Demonstrate improvement to stakeholders
- Create plan for next 30 days (including communication/ change mgt.)

TOLL GATE REVIEW 6: 30-day update to VP and Champion

60 day Results and Follow-up:
- Implement plan from 30 day assessment
- Confirm new process steps with stakeholders
- Collect, analyse and evaluate data
- Demonstrate improvement to stakeholders
- Revise plan for next 30 days (including communication/ change mgt.)

TOLL GATE REVIEW 7: 60-day update to VP and Champion

90 day Results and Follow-up:
- Implement plan from 60 day assessment
- Confirm new process steps with stakeholders
- Collect, analyse and evaluate data
- Demonstrate improvement to stakeholders
- Record new process and create Standard of Work / Update Policies
- Confirm Long-term Sustainability Plan
- Revise communication/ change mgt. plan
- Complete Closure Docs. & Standard Work Documents
- Schedule Report Out with Value Leaders

TOLL GATE REVIEW 8: 90-day VP and Champion approval of Closing Documentation. Approval of sustainability, communications as well as change mgt. plans. Formal approval of Standard of Work.

Project columns: Project 1 | Project 2 | Project 3

Sensei Gyaan: *Whether you use the DMAIC framework, the Lean A3 framework, or a project management body of knowledge framework, develop one standard tollgate process for all project types—department wide or organization wide. Establish standard key milestones at each stage to review the project at the sponsor and senior executive team levels. Display the project status on Wall 3 in the visual strategy room and seek senior management intervention, where required, by highlighting the request on Wall 4 in the visual strategy room.*

Chapter 24

Develop a Five-Year Roadmap and Evaluation Criteria for the Excellence Journey

It's only the last turn of the bolt that tightens it, the rest is just movement.

—Shigeo Shingo

As a leader, it is your responsibility to paint a picture on a blank canvas along with your team of what "good" looks like at the end of a particular period in an excellence journey. The picture of the future has to be compelling enough to create an interest and passion for others to follow. Visionary leaders make people discontent with where they currently are. They inspire people to be courageous, take risks, and endure challenges to get to where they could be. In my experience, five years is a good time horizon to consider in an excellence journey for people to relate, as any shorter period seems overwhelming and stressful, and any longer becomes delusional.

Let's assume, you've got your team energized and you've created an inspiring picture of the future. Now what? At this point people want to know how the rubber hits the road—how we get there from here. Since most people have an operational mindset with a horizon of one year, they want to know what happens year on year for the next five years. The challenge then is to decide whether the design of the roadmap should be based on the number of staff trained, or the number of projects implemented, or something else.

In Chapter 20, I shared the five-year training plan for engaging employees in the More Time to Care journey at Hospital Heal. In Chapter 23, we learned about the tollgate approach for implementing and evaluating projects. Having a standard tollgate process is good, but not good enough. Why? Because implementing projects only addresses the efficiencies and effectiveness part of the operational excellence component in an organization and does not address the bigger aspect—the behavior change component of people, a prerequisite for achieving organizational excellence and culture transformation.

To evaluate movement on the culture change needle, what is required is a maturity scale that defines the levels of maturity in staff behavior that an organization wants to attain over a period of time.

Hospital Heal chose to define its culture change through the adoption of the management system elements in all areas of the organization. The design of the maturity scale included Levels 1 through 4, with the expectation of the employee behavior graduating from learning to applying to aligned, and finally to integrated. The adoption of the management system was defined under three categories, namely, spread, reliability, and sustainability, with each having a specific standard criteria for evaluation (Table 24.1). Standard work observation templates were designed to evaluate the adoption of the management system elements in the organization and corrective measures were undertaken when the adoption level was less than 80%.

An important thing to note here is that the standard work for project sustainability and the standard work for the adoption of the management system to support behavior change have to run synchronously. A bird's

Table 24.1   Standard Work for Adoption of Management System Elements

LEVELS OF BEHAVIOR ADOPTION DEFINE CULTURE CHANGE			
LEVELS OF MATURITY			
LEVEL 1	LEVEL 2	LEVEL 3	LEVEL 4
LEARNING	APPLYING	ALIGNED	INTEGRATED
Behaviors within the process are still incomplete or inconsistent; there is no overall measuring or control	Behaviors show evidence that the process is well understood and implemented	Behaviors are aligned with Standard Work Purpose and Organizational goals	Behaviors are part of daily operations and occurs naturally
SPREAD — 50% of Staff	60% of Staff	70% of Staff	80% of Staff
RELIABILITY — Measurement deferred until Level 4 Spread achieved			80%
SUSTAINABILITY — Measurement deferred until Level 4 Spread achieved			80%

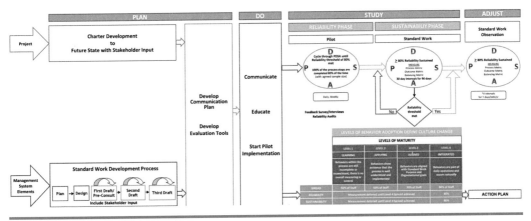

Figure 24.1   Projects and management system elements running synchronously.

eye view of both standards working together at Hospital Heal is shown in Figure 24.1.

Now let's go back and respond to the challenge posed on the roadmap for the excellence journey. In my experience of leading both small- and large-scale change in many organizations across different industries, I have found that developing and implementing a roadmap based on the principles and the elements of the Kumar Management System has been instrumental in successful deployments. Let's understand why adopting the Kumar Management System delivers results. Some of the key reasons, among others, include

- The principles and elements are a compilation from several best-practice frameworks.
- The elements impact all the key categories of business, namely, customers, leadership, strategy, operations, workforce, measurement, information, and knowledge management.
- The combined effect of implementing the twenty-two elements results in sustainable change at an organizational level.
- The model helps break the silo mentality of strategy and operations working in isolation.
- The model establishes focus on changing employee behavior to change organizational culture.
- The simplicity of the model makes it relatable to people at all levels in the organization and makes it a great communication tool.
- The model helps establish a robust structure in the organization to tame the culture beast.

■ The model forces projects, continuous improvement initiatives, and training to work in the background to reinforce the elements supporting behavior change.

■ It sets clear expectations from leaders and staff in the initial crucial years of the excellence journey.

■ The elements can be integrated with employee performance reviews for delivering on organization strategy.

Table 24.2 provides an example of the five-year roadmap developed for the excellence journey at Hospital Heal.

The roadmap clearly laid out the elements to be implemented over the next five years. The plan strategically included elements that would be implemented across all areas of the organization without exception and the additional elements that would be implemented exclusively in the deep dive area (pilot). Since the organization was in an urgent need for transformation to address major internal and external challenges, an aggressive plan was made to undertake the excellence journey with appropriate resource allocation. In the first year, nine out of the twenty-two management system

Table 24.2 Roadmap for the More Time to Care Journey at Hospital Heal

Focus Area	#	CI Sustenance Elements	Year 0	Year 1	Year 2	Year 3	Year 4	Year 5
Patients	1	Patient and Family Partnered Care Practices						
Leadership & Strategy	2	Hospital Report card						
	3	Team Performance Scorecard						
	4	Systems Thinking						
	5	Change Management						
Process	6	Visual Management						
	7	Team-based creative problem solving						
	8	Managing to Demand						
	9	No Meeting Zone						
	10	Go See and Learn						
	11	Daily Status Sheet						
	12	Standard work observation						
	13	Standard work for key unit level processes						
People	14	Education and Coaching						
	15	Team Huddles						
	16	Recognition and development Reviews						
	17	Individual performance Measures						
	18	Leader Standard Work						
	19	Team Report-outs						
Measurement & Information System	20	Monthly Performance Scorecard Review						
	21	Benchmarking and Reflection						
	22	Cross Pollination						

(Year 0 column labeled vertically: "Establish Foundational Elements for the Excellence Journey")

Includes Org wide + Extra for Deep Dive		
Org wide		
Sustainment		

	Year 0	Year 1	Year 2	Year 3	Year 4
Not Planned	6				
Deep Dive	16	22	22	22	22
Org-wide	9	16	22	22	22

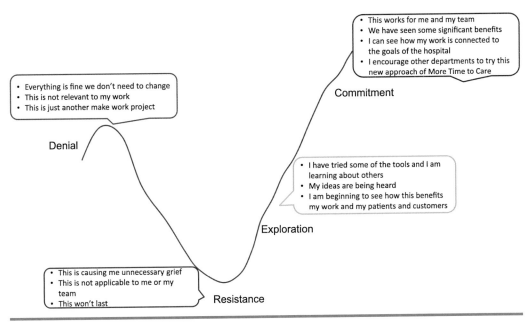

Figure 24.2   Teams at Hospital Heal evolve on the Kübler-Ross change curve.

elements were introduced across the organization and a total of sixteen elements were introduced in the deep dive areas. The implementation of the respective elements became the organization's strategy in the first two years of deployment. This approach created focus in the organization, built momentum, and enabled the organization to cross the threshold needed for change. During the implementation, the teams saw themselves evolve on the Kübler-Ross change curve (Figure 24.2).

Upon reflection, all of us who were involved in the transformation are amazed as to how much we accomplished during the first three years, and how clear strategic direction, relentless focus, appropriate resource allocation, compassionate assertiveness, team execution—all have courageous leadership as their lynchpin, and that's what makes a difference in transforming an organization. The reason Hospital Heal could do nine elements organization wide in the first year is that the CEO and the senior leaders were committed to establishing the key foundational elements required to turn around the organization that was in fiscal and operational crisis, using the philosophy of Lean management. While the commitment to Lean from the CEO and senior leaders continued to remain rock steady over the subsequent years, the pace of implementation and introduction of new elements were strategically reduced to focus on sustaining what had been implemented, and to build an organizational culture of excellence.

Readers are encouraged to draw upon lessons from the real case examples cited, as well as to develop maturity scales and a roadmap for the excellence journey that are meaningful to their respective organizations. Leaders have the option to either show all twenty-two elements of the Kumar Management System together as a big picture to staff or to introduce the elements in phases to not overwhelm their staff. At Hospital Heal, the leadership shared all twenty-two elements with their staff upfront to set clear expectations at an organizational level and more specifically with teams electing to undergo the deep dives (pilot areas).

Sensei Gyaan: *Never underestimate the hidden potential of employees in a crisis situation. Instead, learn to tap into it. Plan the pace of implementation and resource commitment depending on the criticality of the organization's need. Select a maximum of three management system elements for organization-wide implementation in any given year, based on priority. Invest time and resources in building a robust foundation for those elements. Begin implementation.*

Chapter 25

Develop Evaluation Criteria for Selecting a Test Pilot Area for Implementation

Adventure is the child of courage.

—Jonathan Lockwood Huie

Introducing change at an organizational level requires dedication, hard work, grit, persistence, sweat and sometimes tears. There is no elevator to success. You need to take the stairs. The reasons why change is hard include a large scope of change, prohibitive cost, or difficulty in reversing the change and its implications if it does not meet the intended purpose. It is therefore recommended to test pilot the change in select area(s) as a proof of concept before introducing it across the organization. Since the expectation is that the pilot can be replicated easily in other areas of the organization and scaled up fast, the selection of the deep dive area becomes an important consideration for any excellence journey. Just like a sample has to be representative of a population, the deep dive area has to be representative of the organization. Considering that cultures within an organization can vary distinctly, it is good practice to have more than one pilot area for testing the feasibility and reducing the crucial differences between the pilot environment and the environment of the organization as a whole.

At Hospital Heal, the senior leadership team was engaged in identifying the criteria for selecting the deep dive areas. The vice presidents discussed them with the respective directors and managers and critically examined

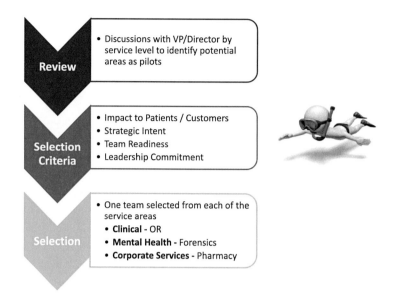

Figure 25.1 **Deep dive selection process at Hospital Heal.**

each of the areas before finalizing the one that best met the selection criteria (Figure 25.1). Since the management system elements to be implemented in the deep dive area were selected before identifying the actual areas for deep dive, the teams electing to undergo the deep dive had a fair sense of what they were getting into.

Team readiness and leadership commitment are absolutely essential in selecting a pilot area. Several best-practice tools for Lean readiness assessment, employee engagement, and operational assessment such as Malcolm Baldrige, Shingo, Gallup, and tools from Todd Sperl's book *Practical Lean Six Sigma for Healthcare*, and David Mann's book, *Creating a Lean Culture*, among many others, were considered for designing the deep dive survey questionnaire. The survey tool administered for the deep dive selection at Hospital Heal is shown in Table 25.1. Results of the survey were analyzed using a radar chart and three teams: one each from clinical, mental health, and corporate were chosen for deep dives.

After the implementation of the first pilot area is complete and learning is incorporated, an organization has the following three options to scale up the change:

1. **Horizontal deployment in a single area:** Change in a new pilot area is implemented one area at a time, until all areas are completed across the organization. Done when the resources to facilitate change are a constraint, customized work effort is needed for implementation

Table 25.1 Example of the Deep Dive Selection Survey at Hospital Heal

Deep Dive Selection Survey	Low → High				
Section 1: Customer Focus					
In my opinion, my department does a good job of listening to and meeting the changing needs/expectations of the customer	1	2	3	4	5
Time spent with patient or customer is seen as most valuable in my area	1	2	3	4	5
We have an established process to receive customer feedback and act on it	1	2	3	4	5
Section 2: Leadership and Strategy					
I am familiar with the organization's strategic directions and understand how my role fits in achieving common goals	1	2	3	4	5
Leaders in my area are actively involved in process improvement to increase time spent with patients or customers	1	2	3	4	5
Managers and supervisors are seen on a regular basis in the work area engaging with the workforce to better understand their reality	1	2	3	4	5
There is a strong sense of trust in the leaders, managers, and associates in my area	1	2	3	4	5
Leadership creates an encouraging and motivating environment and helps staff reach their full potential	1	2	3	4	5
Section 3: Operations					
My department identifies opportunities/gaps in processes on a regular basis	1	2	3	4	5
My department action opportunities and close the gaps in the processes	1	2	3	4	5
Processes in my area are well understood, effective and standardized	1	2	3	4	5
Staff are comfortable to question and/or challenge the status quo	1	2	3	4	5
I have the materials and equipment I need to do my work well	1	2	3	4	5
Section 4: Workforce					
At work, my opinions seem to count	1	2	3	4	5
Staff can openly identify obstacles/problems and seek help in finding solutions	1	2	3	4	5

(Continued)

Table 25.1 (*Continued*) **Example of the Deep Dive Selection Survey at Hospital Heal**

Deep Dive Selection Survey	Low → High				
My associates or fellow employees are consistently committed to do quality work	1	2	3	4	5
I enjoy working with my team	1	2	3	4	5
I am motivated to make improvements and experiment using Lean principles	1	2	3	4	5
Section 5: Measurement, Information and Knowledge Management					
My department makes every effort to ensure data and information are appropriate, accurate, and reliable	1	2	3	4	5
There is a system in place to monitor department progress toward goals and objectives	1	2	3	4	5
It is clear to staff how we use data to improve decision-making	1	2	3	4	5
I use the information collected in reports to guide my daily work	1	2	3	4	5
I understand the reason or importance for the information collected or reports generated in my area	1	2	3	4	5
Thank you for your participation!!!					

Table 25.2 Rule of Thumb to Select a Pilot Area

Staff Readiness to Make Change

Current Situation		Resistant	Indifferent	Ready
Low Confidence that change will lead to improvement	Cost of Failure Large	Don't Select	Don't Select	Not Ideal
	Cost of Failure Small	Don't Select	Not Ideal	Not Ideal
High Confidence that change will lead to improvement	Cost of Failure Large	Don't Select	Not Ideal	Select
	Cost of Failure Small	Not Ideal	Select	Select

in every area, and the organization is stable and has no time crunch to spread the change.

2. **Horizontal deployment in multiple areas:** Change is implemented in multiple pilot areas across the organization in waves or phases. Done when the resources to facilitate change can be made available, heavy customization among work areas is not required, and the organization is stable and feels the need to spread the change faster than doing it one area at a time.

3. **Jing Bang:** This is the organization-wide implementation without any further pilots. Jing Bang is done when the organization is in survival mode and has an urgent need to transform. It requires concentrated effort and focus, significant resources, and a high pace of implementation for a limited time period.

Sensei Gyaan: *Practitioners and leaders can use Table 25.2 as a rule of thumb to select pilot area(s) in their organization. Create visibility, celebrate initial success stories, and acknowledge individuals and teams. Let leaders and staff in the pilot areas promote the benefits of implementation to their peers in nonpilot areas to create a pull effect. Continue to invest in training and leadership development and build momentum until you cross the threshold required for change to be successful.*

Chapter 26

Develop Individual Performance Measures for Leaders to Build Accountability

Tell me how you measure me and I will tell you how I'll behave. Measurements drive behavior. If you do not have the right measurements, you have no right to expect the right behavior.

—Dr. Eli Goldratt

In the sequence of building the foundation for change, this is the final element to build after all other foundational elements have been developed. The reason why we do this at the end is because it provides leaders an opportunity to consider performance metrics that could arise from any of the previous foundational elements before finalizing the individual performance measures (IPMs), also commonly known as individual key performance indicators (KPIs) or individual key result areas (KRAs). In the words of Eiji Toyoda, former president and chairman of Toyota Motor Corporation, "Employees are offering a very important part of their own life to us. If we don't use their time effectively, we are wasting their lives."

It is common practice in many organizations to develop IPMs having a mix of quantitative and qualitative measures cascaded directly from the balanced scorecard or having project deliverables tied to an individual's performance.

Also, some organizations use an appraisal system based on employee job descriptions, a 360-degree feedback, employee engagement scores to formulate IPMs. This approach is good for delivering very specific short-term goals but not appropriate for the long haul, especially when transforming organizational culture is the mandate. Why? Because people express their values through personal behaviors and organizations express their values through cultural behaviors.
A recent survey report published by Boston Consulting Group confirms that organizations driven by purpose and values outperform their competitors in revenue, profit, and stock performance. Jon Katzenbach, founder of the Katzenbach Centre, says, "Instead of changing culture significantly, it is much better to change the behaviors because they are more tangible and measurable. Cultures don't change automatically, but they do tend to follow behavior change."

While there is enough evidence to support the role of individual behavior in an organizational excellence and culture transformation, not much has been done to develop individual performance measures that promote ideal behavior to change organizational culture. Isadore Sharp, founder and chairman of Four Season Hotels and Resorts, said, "You can write the metrics on a paper, but they are only words…The words have significance only if behaved. Behaviors have significance only if believed."

Before I share examples of IPMs developed for Hospital Heal to promote behavior change, I would like to share two popular models/frameworks and a scorecard template that focus on individual behavioral characteristics and leadership attributes for achieving enterprise excellence.

A. **The Shingo Model™:** Developed by the Shingo Institute, one of the pioneers in incorporating culture in their excellence model. The model provides the following three insights (Figure 26.1):
   i. Ideal results require ideal behaviors
   ii. Beliefs and systems drive behavior
   iii. Principles inform ideal behavior
The Shingo Model™ of operational excellence is built on the foundation of cultural enablers that includes the principles of (1) lead with humility and (2) respect every individual—both qualities of a great organization. In the early 2000s, the philosopher Theodore Zeldin said, "When will we make the same breakthroughs in the way we treat each other as we have made in technology?" It is said that kindness is the language that the deaf can hear and the blind can see. The Shingo Model™ asserts that successful organizational transformation occurs when leaders understand and take personal responsibility for architecting a deep

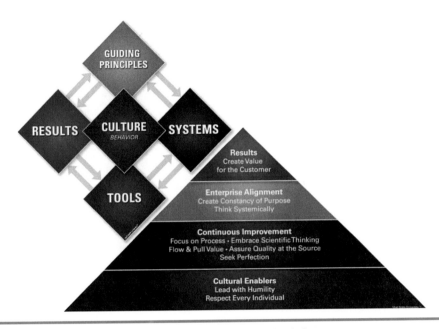

Figure 26.1 The Shingo Model™ and its guiding principles.

and abiding culture of continuous improvement. Leaders anchor the corporate mission, vision, and values in principles of operational excellence and help associates to connect and anchor their personal values in the same principles. They accelerate a transformation of thinking and behavior and therefore create a lasting culture of operational excellence. In his article on operational excellence, Robert Miller, former executive director of the Shingo Institute, says, "Improvement cannot be delegated down, organized into a program or trained into the people. Improvement requires more than the application of a new tool set or the power of a charismatic personality. Improvement requires the transformation of a culture to one where every single person is engaged every day in often small and from time to time, significant change."

B. **Competing Values Framework:** Developed by Kim S. Cameron and Robert E. Quinn, both professors at the University of Michigan, for diagnosing and changing organizational culture, this framework provides a distinct set of skills for leaders and managers that are most effective in each of the four quadrants (Figure 26.2) for moving an organization to its desired culture. The framework has proven to be very robust in describing the core approaches to thinking, behaving, and organizing associated with human activity.

C. **Marshall Goldsmith's mojo scorecard:** Dr. Marshall Goldsmith is one of the world's leading executive educators and coaches. In his book, *What*

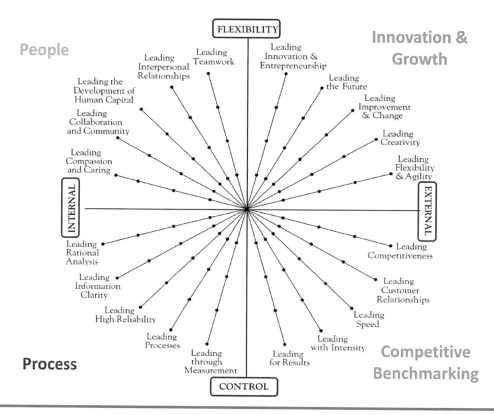

Figure 26.2 Skills profile for leaders based on the Competing Values Framework. (Cameron, K.S. and R.E. Quinn. *Diagnosing and Changing Organizational Culture: Based on the Competing Values Framework.* San Francisco: Jossey-Bass, 2010.)

Got You Here Won't Get You There, he says, "People will do something—including changing their behavior—only if it can be demonstrated that doing so is in their own best interests as defined by their own values." In his other book, *Mojo,* Marshall provides a scorecard that helps measure the two forms of mojo in our lives: professional mojo and personal mojo (Table 26.1). He defines mojo as the moment when we do something that's purposeful, powerful, and positive and the rest of the world recognizes it.

The goal is to increase the overall mojo score (maximum 100), which is dependent on ten equally weighted elements, five elements each in the professional and personal categories as detailed below.

Elements of professional Mojo: What I bring to this activity

■ Motivation: How engaged do I feel about the activity?
■ Knowledge: Do I understand what to do?
■ Ability: Do I have the skills to do the task well?

Table 26.1 Dr. Marshall Goldsmith's Mojo Scorecard

ACTIVITY	PROFESSIONAL MOJO						PERSONAL MOJO						MOJO SCORE
	MOTIVATION	KNOWLEDGE	ABILITY	CONFIDENCE	AUTHENTICITY	TOTAL	HAPPINESS	REWARDS	MEANING	LEARNING	GRATITUDE	TOTAL	
1.													
2.													
3.													
4.													
5.													
6.													
7.													
8.													
9.													
10.													
11.													
12.													
13.													
14.													

- Confidence: How sure am I of myself?
- Authenticity: Is my enthusiasm genuine?

Elements of personal Mojo: What this activity brings to me

- Happiness: Am I happy when engaged in this activity?
- Reward: Does this activity provide me with material or emotional rewards?
- Meaning: Are the results of this activity meaningful to me?
- Learning: Does this activity help me learn and grow?
- Gratitude: Do I feel grateful for this activity, and is it a great use of my time?

It is a good tool to validate and prioritize your daily activities. Used creatively, you can replace the activities with management system elements in an excellence journey and check the mojo score for your leaders and their teams.

The guidelines and frameworks shared above are examples to trigger the reader's thinking process for identifying measures and developing IPMs that build accountability and to inspire the leadership mindset, "Improving the work is the work."

Excellence is an art won by training and habituation. We do not act rightly because we have virtue or excellence, but we rather have

*those because we have acted rightly. We are what we repeatedly do.
Excellence, then, is not an act but a habit.*

—Aristotle

Transformational change is more than fine-tuning the status quo with a redesign of systems and processes. Transformational change requires people to reframe how they think about and perceive their roles, responsibilities, and relationships. Having IPMs designed around the balanced scorecard outcome measures makes it merely an act, visited only a few times in a year, and does not hold leaders accountable to repeat the act on a daily basis to make it a habit. As Jalal ad-Din Rumi said, "Yesterday I was clever, so I wanted to change the world. Today I am wise, so I am changing myself."

Table 26.2 provides examples of the IPMs developed for the leaders at Hospital Heal that promoted behavior change. After considering several

Table 26.2 **Example of Individual Performance Measures for Leaders at Hospital Heal**

Individual Performance Metrics for CEO, Vice Presidents, Directors, and Managers						
Category	#	CEO + Vice Presidents	#	Directors	#	Managers
Patient and Family	1	# of Patient and/or Customer Stories shared formally	1	# of Patient and/or Customer Stories shared formally		
Leadership and Strategy	2	# of Performance Scorecard Reviews conducted				
Process	3	# of Go See Learns completed	2	# of Go See Learns completed		
			3	# of huddles attended	1	# of huddles attended
People	4	% of RDRs completed that are due	4	% of RDRs completed that are due	2	% of RDRs completed that are due
			5	Individual Learning Plan completed	3	Individual Learning Plan completed
Initiative	5	Lead on QIP initiative(s)				

Note: RDR = Recognition and Developmental Review; QIP = Quality Improvement Plan

options, elements of the management system were chosen to operational-ize the desired behaviors for creating a new culture. The measures were integrated with their recognition and development review (RDR) appraisal system, and continuous coaching and feedback interactions replaced bien-nial (once in two years) formal reviews.

Sensei Gyaan: *Undertake culture assessment. Find the gap between the current state and the desired future state of culture. Leverage strengths of your current culture and identify behavioral characteristics that support in implementing your organizational strategy. Think KBI (Key Behavior Indicators) vs KPI (Key Performance Indicators). Select KBIs that support those behavioral characteristics to get the desired results.*

LEADERSHIP AND COURAGE

F

A ship is safe in harbor, but that is not what ships are made for.

—William G. T. Shedd

The first five parts (twenty-six chapters) of this book are dedicated to building the foundation for implementing transformational change. However, Lean principles, systems, and structures cannot be delivered in the absence of leadership demonstrating courage to withstand adversities along the transformational change journey. Leadership takes courage! As Winston Churchill said, "Success is not final, and failure is not fatal: it is the courage to continue that counts." In this section, I am going to share excerpts of leadership and courage, and contextualize their role in an organizational excellence and culture transformation journey.

In their book, *Bringing Leadership to Life in Health: LEADS in a Caring Environment*, Graham Dickson and Bill Tholl describe leadership as energy, influence, perseverance, dedication, strategy, and execution, applied in the world of people to create change. Leadership works through activities, approaches, and strategies to engage the will and commitment of individuals and professional groups to work together to bring meaningful change.

Stephen Covey differentiates between "Management" and "Leadership." He says, "Management is efficiency in climbing the ladder of success; leadership determines whether the ladder is leaning against the right wall." Management is working "IN" the system. Leadership is working "ON" the system. Management cares about efficiency. Leadership cares about people. Simon Sinek says, "Leadership is not about being in charge. Leadership is about taking care of those in your charge." In the same note, Sheryl

Table F1.1   **Twenty Behavioral Capabilities of Leaders Identified in the LEADS Framework**

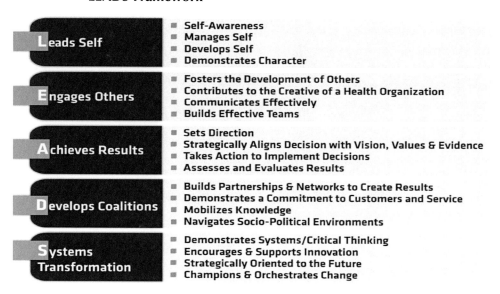

Leads Self	■ Self-Awareness ■ Manages Self ■ Develops Self ■ Demonstrates Character
Engages Others	■ Fosters the Development of Others ■ Contributes to the Creative of a Health Organization ■ Communicates Effectively ■ Builds Effective Teams
Achieves Results	■ Sets Direction ■ Strategically Aligns Decision with Vision, Values & Evidence ■ Takes Action to Implement Decisions ■ Assesses and Evaluates Results
Develops Coalitions	■ Builds Partnerships & Networks to Create Results ■ Demonstrates a Commitment to Customers and Service ■ Mobilizes Knowledge ■ Navigates Socio-Political Environments
Systems Transformation	■ Demonstrates Systems/Critical Thinking ■ Encourages & Supports Innovation ■ Strategically Oriented to the Future ■ Champions & Orchestrates Change

Sandberg says, "Leadership is about making others better as a result of your presence and making sure that impact lasts in your absence." Leadership is about humanity and humility, and in the words of Michael Jordon, "You have to earn your leadership every day."

The LEADS in a Caring Environment leadership capabilities framework (Table F1.1) represents the key skills, abilities, and knowledge required to lead at all levels of an organization. It identifies twenty capabilities under five domains for transformational leaders. Leaders tailor action on these capabilities and exemplify behaviors according to their own individual strengths, weaknesses, and character. Embodying the collective wisdom of the current literature on leadership and leadership development in the Canadian health sector, the LEADS framework is comparable to the top leadership competency frameworks in the private, public, and health sectors around the world.

Lisa Dungate and Jennifer Armstrong in their blog Lion's Whiskers (www.lionswhiskers.com) categorize courage into six types (Figure F1.1).

1. Physical: Facing a challenge involving the risk of physical injury or death
2. Social: Standing up for oneself or others despite the risk of alienating others
3. Moral: Doing the right thing, despite the risk of opposition or loss of status
4. Emotional: Opening oneself to unpleasant emotions
5. Intellectual: Opening oneself to ideas that differ from one's own opinions
6. Spiritual: Facing up to the uncertainty of the purpose for one's existence

Physical

Spiritual   Social

Intellectual   Moral

Emotional

Figure F1.1   **Six categories of Courage.**

Paul Zygielbaum, author of *Management Lessons from Oz*, is also influenced by Lion's Whiskers. He defines courage as willingness to act, despite fear. Fear delimits our ability to lead. Courage, hope, and conviction drive leadership and action.

Peter F. Drucker, founder of modern management, wrote that the purpose of strategy is to enable an organization to achieve its desired results in an unpredictable environment. Contrary to what "everybody knows," strategy is not about achieving results in a known and foreseeable environment, but in an environment that is unknown and unforeseeable. Therefore, in business and in healthcare, leaders need moral, social, emotional, and intellectual courage. I am sharing below select content on these categories of courage from the exceptionally informative and well-researched blog Lion's Whiskers.

While leaders can fall into any category, the most challenging situations are those that call for moral courage. In his book *The Mystery of Courage*, William Ian Miller, a professor at the University of Michigan Law School, writes, "The thing that distinguishes moral courage from all other forms of courage is that it is usually *a lonely courage*." Leaders, especially those at the top and those who are called upon to make bold, crucial, unpopular, and often brutal decisions that impact the lives of many people, sometimes find themselves lonely and challenged. Courage is having the strength of conviction to do the right thing when it would just be easier to do things right.

Courage is what it takes to stand up and speak; courage is also what it takes to sit down and listen.

—Winston Churchill

Social courage is standing up tall, being able to greet the world with your head held high, feeling comfortable in your own skin. Social courage means not conforming to the expectations of others, being willing to show your true self even if it means risking social disapproval or punishment. It means being able to express opinions and preferences without checking to see if they are in line with "everyone else's" opinions and preferences. Mahatma Gandhi said, "It's easy to stand in a crowd. It takes courage to stand alone."

Emotional courage is the willingness to be vulnerable, truthful, and aware of your conscious experience of core emotions, which you think about and express often in language as feelings. When we choose to ignore, suppress, or deny our emotion, we risk a reduction of insight, leading to faulty decision making and inaccurate mental representation of our experience. Emotional courage also means loving yourself, being proud of yourself, and believing that you are worthy of love and happiness. Essentially, it is related to self-acceptance, coupled with a willingness to move outside of our comfort zone, to explore new ways of being that may not be familiar. Barbara A. Trautlein, author of *Change Intelligence*, believes that powerful change leaders start with the heart, engage the brain, and help the hands move in positive new directions.

Courage makes change possible. Intellectual courage is necessary to challenge conventional wisdom and imagine new possibilities: a new way to lead and a new way to manage in a completely new business model. Intellectual courage means grappling with difficult or confusing concepts, asking questions, struggling to gain understanding, and risking mistakes. Integrity and authenticity are interwoven with intellectual courage. As Mary Anne Radmacher says, "Courage doesn't always roar. Sometimes courage is the little voice that says I'll try again tomorrow."

Steve Jobs, cofounder of Apple Inc., articulated, "You can't connect the dots looking forward; you can only connect them looking backwards. So you have to trust that the dots will somehow connect in your future. You have to trust in something—your gut, destiny, life, karma, whatever. Because believing that the dots will connect down the road will give you the confidence to follow your heart, even when it leads you off the well-worn path."

David Silverstein, CEO of Lean Methods Group, highlights in Figure F1.2 the zone where courageous leaders are comfortable taking action despite the lack of all information.

Arlene Dickson, managing partner of District Venture Capital, says, "There are no perfect answers to business and life's questions. Sometimes you just gotta pick your best possible guess answer. If you wait for

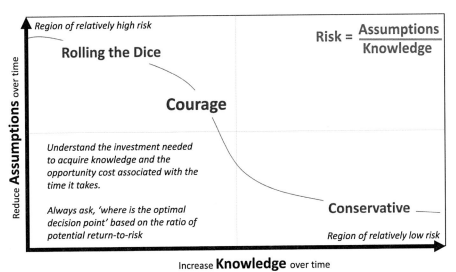

Figure F1.2   **The assumption-to-knowledge ratio.**

everything to be perfect before you decide you will be waiting a long, long time. So take smart leaps of faith. Arm yourself with the best info you can gather at the time, a bit of gut instinct and a belief that if your choice doesn't work out exactly how you want it to, you can take another run at it. This time a bit smarter."

Missed opportunities lead to regrets later. As Wayne Gretzky said, "You miss 100 percent of the shots you don't take." Every industry has a Kodak moment, when disruption radically changed their business model. Nokia could have innovated its way to dominance in smartphones. Yahoo could have sold to Microsoft. But they didn't. In the words of Yogi Berra, "When you come to a fork in the road, take it." Facebook, Google, Airbnb, and many other web-based firms are only a few years old and worth billions of dollars. In fact, Airbnb founded in as recent as 2008, is now the world's biggest accommodation provider with 1.5 million individual properties around the world. The answer lies in being nimble and fast. Robert Frost said, "Two roads diverged in a wood … I took the one less travelled by, and that has made all the difference." As a leader, are you watching and prepared?

Margie Warrell, in her book *Stop Playing Safe*, provides a simple yet powerful framework (Figure F1.3) on how leaders lead in today's increasingly competitive, accelerated, and uncertain world. First, the leader engages authentically with people to build trust. Second, the leader enlarges the context and helps employees understand the bigger "why." Third, leaders demonstrate courage to unleash the human potential within their teams and

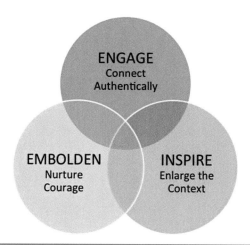

Figure F1.3 **Margie Warrell's framework for leaders in *Stop Playing Safe.***

organization, tap ingenuity, raise the bar on innovation, and optimize the value their organization contributes to *all* of its stakeholders. She says, "It doesn't take the brains of an Einstein to do that, but it does take the heart of a lion." In the words of Alexander the Great, "I am not afraid of an army of lions led by a sheep; I am afraid of an army of sheep led by a lion."

Needless to say, all leadership is a function of time, place, and circumstance, so a leadership framework has to be adaptable and responsive to the situation. Also, leadership is not a function of the power of an individual's position in an organization but rather of the power inherent in an individual's ability to influence others. In his book, *The Circle of Innovation*, Tom Peters writes, "We are all Michelangelos—Michelangelos of housekeeping; Michelangelos of parking; Michelangelos of accounts receivable; Michelangelos of plumbing; Michelangelos of selling; Michelangelos of hairstyling; Michelangelos of _ _ _ _ _ _ _? (You fill in the blanks.) Choose to come to work with a Michelangelo attitude." Likewise, in the story of the barnyard breakfast which the chicken and the pig agree to co-host, the chicken suggests that they serve bacon and eggs. The pig replies, "For you it means involvement. For me it's total commitment."

In an organization needing turnaround, or pursuing excellence and culture transformation, you need Michelangelos with pig commitment. In short, Gung Ho employees committed to success. Leaders have the responsibility to create an environment for the Gung Ho Michelangelos to thrive. Leaders decide what position team members play but then get off the field and let the payers move the ball. The Lean management system provides the structure to create such an environment. Courage provides

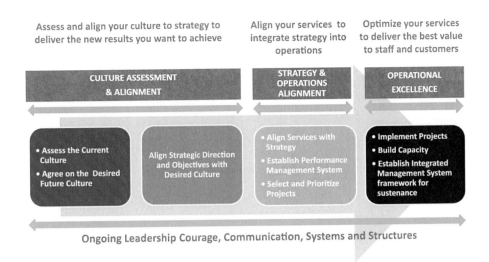

Figure F1.4   An approach to an organizational excellence culture.

the fuel in leaders that makes them resilient to repeated failures and persistent in driving implementation. Matthew Syed, in his book *Bounce*, writes, "Excellence is about stepping outside the comfort zone, training with a spirit of endeavour, and accepting the inevitability of trials and tribulations. Progress is built, in effect, upon the foundations of necessary failure." Transformations and excellence journeys fail because one of these two essentials, namely, the environment and courage, are either missing or lacking. Some begin with all the right ingredients but lose momentum along the way, mostly because the fuel of courage in leadership became depleted during tough times or while facing resistance to change.

To disrupt the status quo, to create success in an uncertain, ambiguous, volatile, and complex business environment that increasingly demands speed to respond, to take action, to say no, to make decisions, to be compassionately assertive, to have the tenacity to hold people to high standards, to create value, and to engage stakeholders in constructive and meaningful ways, while being patient, humble, respectful, resilient, and confident in the process, courage is needed. Period.

Only when employees see "improving the work" as their work, integrate Lean management principles into their daily operations, and build trust with their leaders who back their daily experiments to make things better will an organization experience transformation to a Lean culture. Courageous leadership is, therefore, "The Missing Link to Creating a Lean Culture of Excellence." A roadmap to creating an organizational excellence culture is shared in Figure F1.4.

Annexure

Annexure 1

Making the Most of Meetings Standard Work – Chairing Meetings			
Last Updated:		**Performed By:**	Chairs of committees, work groups
Revision:		**Frequency:**	N/A
Standard Work Owner:	Any person chairing a meeting at Hospital Heal	**Duration:**	As per meeting agenda
Standard Work Purpose: To provide standard guidelines on chairing meetings to ensure maximum participation and effectiveness of meetings.			
Guidelines for Chairing a Meeting			

1. Before the Meeting

- Make every meeting matter – or don't meet at all. Decide if a meeting is needed and invite the necessary people.
- Plan the agenda – decide the order and timing of each item, which items are for information, discussion or decision.
- When sending the meeting invitation, attach the agenda, previous minutes and all necessary documents beforehand.
- Determine a "cut-off" for receiving agenda items in order to set one agenda, and avoid multiple versions and distributions.
- Confirm guests and all relevant equipment and room set up ahead of time.
- Arrive in good time before the meeting is to start.

2. During the Meeting

- Own your meeting – take charge and keep it moving forward.
- Start on time and make necessary introductions, ensuring the recorder has the names and information about all attendees.
- Set the scene – put everyone on the same page by stating the meeting's objectives.
- Limit adding new items – they will extend your meeting – decide what's acceptable and relevant to add, and table others for another time.
- Make it clear you intend to keep the discussion timely and balance this with some freedom of expression.
- Guide the discussion to stay on topic – if the conversation starts to drift, refocus the group.
- Draw out constructive input and check in to make sure all is clear and understood.
- Avoid dismissing ideas – encourage diverse perspectives – expect, respect and accept disagreements.
- Invest a few minutes to summarize decisions and action points to be followed – the reward will be concise and quality minutes.
- Close with an action plan – make sure everyone leaves knowing next steps and don't hesitate to check in with your colleagues about the quality and effectiveness of your meeting.

Annexure 1.1

Making the Most of Meetings Standard Work – Participating in Meetings			
Last Updated:		**Performed By:**	Any participants of committees, workgroups
Revision:		**Frequency:**	N/A
Standard Work Owner:	Any person attending a meeting at Hospital Heal	**Duration:**	As per meeting agenda

Standard Work Purpose: To provide standard guidelines on participating in meetings to ensure effectiveness of meetings and attaining the identified goals.

Guidelines for Participating in Meetings

1. Be Present at Meetings

- Meetings will begin and end on time. Endeavour to inform the Chair ahead of time if you foresee arriving late or having to leave early.
- Come prepared. Preview agenda and attachments. If you are on the agenda, be ready to give a concise report.
- Ensure items that you add to the agenda are relevant to the majority of the group. Otherwise, plan to discuss with stakeholders at a separate time.
- If you wish to invite a guest, check with the Chair prior to the meeting.
- Electronics: Avoid multitasking, as it prevents focus. Minimize use of mobile phones and laptops. Understanding that there may be a need to respond to time-sensitive matters, be discreet – avoid clicking keys on your laptop or phone.
- Silence phones and laptops during meetings.
- Avoid side conversations.
- When speaking, be concise using clear terms; avoid acronyms. When on tele/videoconference, be sure to speak close to the microphone.
- Listen. Do not interrupt; avoid blurting out comments or questions. Signal to the Chair that you wish to speak, or raise your hand to be recognized by the Chair.
- All meeting participants share the responsibility for making meetings successful by being active, respectful and responsive.

Annexure 2

IDEAS/HOW MIGHT WE...?	EXPERIMENTS

IDEAS/HOW MIGHT WE...?

Name: _____ Date: _____

Problem: _____

_____

_____

Idea: _____

_____

_____

Expected Benefits: _____

_____

_____

Strategic Direction *(Circle one)*:

      Access   Partnerships   People   Wise Choices

Metric: _____

Owner _____

Complete Date _____

MORE TIME TO CARE

EXPERIMENTS

Next Steps: _____

_____

_____

_____

_____

_____

Actions Completed: _____

_____

_____

_____

_____

_____

_____

_____

MORE TIME TO CARE

Standard IDEA Card at the Hospital Heal

Annexure 3

Standard Work for Huddles			
Last Updated:		**Performed By:**	Any team member
Revision:		**Frequency:**	Daily to Weekly
Standard Work Owner:	Manager	**Huddle Duration:**	15 minutes

Standard Work Purpose: To provide all care team members an opportunity to come together on a regular basis to overcome daily operational challenges, prioritize issues and celebrate experiments.

PLAN

Ensure the metric data is populated and up to date. Post any celebrations and support requests.

DO

1. Start Huddle Timer

Welcome Team and Guests to the Huddle

2. Review Work in Progress

Ask the project owner to provide an update. Ensure the back of the card is completed.
Ask "How Might We...?" to help overcome any challenges.
Write any ideas on an Idea/How Might We...? card and place in the Ideas section.

3. Review How Can We Help

Review all collaboration requests. Address as a team or escalate as appropriate.
Ask if there are any issues in the department that you need help with or that need to be escalated?

4. Review Just Do Its

Move completed items to the Implemented column and celebrate!

5. Review Ideas/How Might We...?

Ask the idea generator to share their idea.
    Prioritize ideas using the PICK chart
Ask: Does this idea require high or low effort?
    Does it have a small or big impact?
Identify Just Do It ideas. Assign an owner to experiment with the idea and collaborate with the team.
Reminder: The Huddle is not used to find solutions. It is a time to brainstorm ideas, seek advice, deploy resources, or ask for support.
Ask the team: "Are there any other ideas?" Write them down on Idea/How Might We...? Card

6. Celebrate

End on a high note: Identify and celebrate work and projects implemented, accomplishments, thank you notes, good news, patient/staff compliments, and make them visual.

STUDY

The Manager, Director and Senior Leader share and discuss their learnings and observations from the Huddles during the Monthly Scorecard Reviews.

ADJUST

Increase frequency of Huddles as needed. Through experimentation, your learnings will influence your next Huddle.

Annexure 4

Standard Work for No Meeting Zone			
Date:		**Performed by:**	Managers, Directors, Senior Leadership Team
Revision:		**Frequency:**	Daily to Weekly
Standard Work Owner:	Managers, Directors, Senior Leadership Team	**Duration:**	2 hours

Standard Work Purpose: To provide regular protected time for supporting all activities that help improve the patient and customer experience. This time will be used to *Go See Learn* where the processes are taking place, attend Huddles, educate, mentor, coach, have Daily or Weekly Status conversations, and champion leader standard work.

PLAN

1. Book No Meeting Zone Time

All management team members will ensure they have two hours of No Meeting Zone time protected in their calendar at least once a week to support the work described in the 'Standard Work Purpose'.

DO

2. Select Activity

Take time to select one or more of the following activities for the No Meeting Zone:

- *Go See Learn:*
  a. *Patient Conversation Worksheet*
  b. *Process Observation Worksheet*
  c. *Staff Conversation Worksheet*
- *Daily/Weekly Status Sheet*
- *Huddle*
- *Educate, Mentor, and Coach*

STUDY

3. Evaluate

Regularly participate in the evaluation of the frequency of the No Meeting Zone and increase activities that support the patient and customer experience.

ADJUST

The interactions with staff, patients and families, and customers will begin to influence your No Meeting Zone.

Annexure 5

Standard Work for Go See Learn			
Last Updated:		**Performed By:**	Managers, Directors, Vice Presidents/Medical Directors, CEO (Senior Leadership Team)
Revision:		**Frequency:**	Weekly
Standard Work Owner:	Managers, Directors, Vice Presidents/Medical Directors/CEO (Senior Leadership Team)	**Duration:**	During No Meeting Zone time

Standard Work Purpose: To provide Managers, Directors and Senior Leadership Team an opportunity to go where the work happens, to observe and learn while interacting with staff/patients and families to better understand our business. Through observations and respectful conversations, the Go See Learn provides an opportunity to enhance lines of communication, establish trust and collaboration, and recognize accomplishments.

PLAN

1. Prepare for Go See Learn

Check your calendar for No Meeting Zone and schedule your time between all areas you support
Review the data that your scorecard area supports
Data sources include but are not limited to:
  - *Performance Scorecard Metric Data*
  - *Incident Report (REDS)*
  - *Compliments and Complaints*
  - *Audit Reports*
  - *Benchmarking Data*
  - *Federal and Provincial Reports*
  - *Survey Results (Accreditation, Patient and Family Partnered Care)*
The data will direct you to the process you need to observe and learn.

Select one or more of the following worksheets:
  a. *Patient Conversation Worksheet*
  b. *Process Observation Worksheet*
  c. *Staff Conversation Worksheet*

DO

2. Go See Learn

Begin your Go See Learn where the process is taking place. Observe and have conversations with staff, patients and families to understand what is working well and what is not working well.

Remember to:
Respectfully ask staff "Tell me more" and "Explain a little further" *in order to peel away layers of assumptions and probe deeper. Focus on listening.*
Resist the urge *to give solutions immediately. Ask why and/or open-ended questions, 'How Might We…?' to guide staff through the problem-solving process.*

(Continued)

STUDY
3. Reflect and Share
The Manager, Director and Senior Leader share and discuss their learnings and their observations during Huddles, Monthly Scorecard Reviews, and Status Sheets.
ADJUST
Through experimentation, your learnings will influence your next Go See Learn.
GUIDELINES

Tone:
- *Respectful*
- *Supportive, safe environment to share information*
- *Clear and Concise*
- *Motivating*
- *Shared Accountability*

Think of the acronym **GIFTS** to achieve the most out of the Go See Learn:

Good start - Good Start means protecting your time for the Go See Learn and gearing up for activities that support the standard work purpose.

Improvement - We can't fix problems we don't know about. The Go See Learn provides a venue to understand gaps in our processes that are bottlenecks and reduce flow through the system. Improvement is not just about problem solving, it's about experimentation, idea generation and shared learning.

Focus - It is too easy to confuse effort with work. The Go See Learn instills a clear sense of purpose and creates a sense of urgency to achieve our objectives.

Team - Effective teams are built by regularly communicating, working together, and helping each other with shared obstacles.

Status - Status is the ability to answer the following three questions:
- *What's working well?*
- *What's not working well?*
- *What support does the team need?*

Annexure 5.1

Go See Learn: Standard Patient Conservation Worksheet		
Area:		**Date:**
I am taking feedback from: Patient X Family Member ☐ A.B.		

	Conversation Questions	**Reflections – What I Learned**
Go Listen	What's working well for you?	
	What's not working well for you?	*Med Mixed this morning.* *- TO DO: Do process* *observation on Med Rec* *Project*
	Are you being given **clear information** about your care? Yes ☐ No X	*Didn't get Fall Prevention* *documentation at Admit.* *TO DO: F/u at Huddle* *tomorrow*
	Are you being treated with **dignity and respect**? Yes X No ☐	*Kudos on Huddle*
	Are you or your family **involved** in your care to the level you wanted? Yes ☐ No ☐	
	Are you satisfied with your overall care experience? Yes ☐ No ☐	
	What can we do differently to improve your experience today?	
	Is there any staff in particular that you would like to recognize or tell me about? Yes X No ☐	*Recognize Sheila for her* *outstanding care in C3.27* *on Jan 7th*
	Observation Questions	**Reflections – What I Learned**
Go See	What do you observe is working well for patients and families?	
	What do you observe is not working well for patients and families?	
	What would you recommend to improve the patient experience?	
Actionable Items:		
☑ Bring opportunities and recognitions to Huddle		

TIPS:
- Resist the urge to give solutions immediately
- Respectfully ask "*Tell me more*" and "*Explain a little further*" in order to peel away layers of assumptions and probe deeper
- Focus on listening
- Inform patient and family member about the formal survey

Annexure 5.2

Go See Learn: Standard Process Observation Worksheet				
The Process I will observe today: *Medication Reconciliation*			**Date:**	
Rationale: *Medication Reconciliation – as near med error input in REDS And part of PSC Metric*				
	DOWNTIME		**Description**	**Example**	**Waste observed and follow up**
Observation	**Defect**		Any patient care or work activity not done right the first time.	Omission of pain medication as scheduled.	*Second source not documented*
	Overproduction		Doing work earlier than needed by the customer, or doing work that is not needed.	Assembling a dietary tray for a patient who has been discharged.	*2 Staff started BPMH – ? lack communication ? no visual cue*
	Waiting		Time when nothing is happening (when productive activity *could be* happening).	• In a waiting room • For a bed to be available • For order to be written or processed	*Took 45 mins to receive fax from Community Pharmacy.*
	Non-utilized talent		Not utilizing employee's inherent talent, skills, and abilities.	Failing to seek and listen to ideas for improvement.	
	Transportation		Excess movement of patients through the hospital.	Transferring patients to new rooms or units.	
	Inventory		Holding too much or too little material to efficiently perform the work.	• Overstock items expiring on the shelf • Under stock supplies delaying surgical procedures	
	Motion		Excess motion required by employees to get the work done.	Walking excessively to assemble supplies due to poor layout or design.	
	Extra-processing		Doing more work than necessary for good patient care or for the customer needs.	Duplicating electronic medical record information on paper.	

(Continued)

<table>
<tr><td rowspan="3" style="writing-mode: vertical">Conversations</td><td>

What's working well?

Pharm tech verified meds with Pt
Pt brought in there meds to clarify confusion
New flagging system for physician being noticed

</td></tr>
<tr><td>

What's not working well?

</td></tr>
</table>

Actionable Items:
Speak to Kathryn Dsouza Re: other units process

☑ Bring opportunities and recognitions to Huddle

TIPS:
- Resist the urge to give solutions immediately
- Respectfully ask "*Tell me more*" and "*Explain a little further*" in order to peel away layers of assumptions and probe deeper
- Focus on listening

Annexure 5.3

Go See Learn: Standard Staff Conversation Worksheet		
Area:		**Date:**
Focus Today: *Morale and Team Work*		
	Observation Questions	**Reflections – What I Learned**
Go See	What do you observe is working well?	
	What do you observe is not working well?	
	What is the energy in the department?	
	Are staff helping each other?	
	Conversation Questions	**Reflections – What I Learned**
Go Listen	What's working well for you?	
	What's not working well for you?	
	How do you orient new staff?	
	How would you like to be recognized?	
	Tell me about a typical day.	

Actionable Items:

☑ Bring opportunities and recognitions to Huddle

TIPS:
• Resist the urge to give solutions immediately
• Respectfully ask *"Tell me more"* and *"Explain a little further"* in order to peel away layers of assumptions and probe deeper

Annexure 5.4

Go See Learn: Sample Conversation Starter Questions – Patient Safety
What is the process of addressing a safety issue in your area?
Help me better understand the challenges you face on a daily basis? Tell me more about some of the challenges you face regarding patient safety... Share some of your ideas to improve patient safety in your area. What are staff and leaders at all levels doing well to promote a patient safety climate, and what can we do better? How can we ensure patient safety is considered in all decisions? When you are having a busy day, how do you continue to deliver high quality, safe care?
How do you like to be recognized? How could we promote good catches in our area? Is there a process for bringing forward safety ideas in your area? Share some of your ideas to improve patient safety in our area.
Think of an incident that occurred in your area. How would you prevent the same mistake in the future?
What type of incidents would you typically report in REDS? Are there any safety issues that you have reported and have not yet been addressed? What is the process when you witness or learn about an incident?
How might we make it safe to discuss errors? Tell me how I could help you overcome your fear of experimentation. The huddles boards have 'Experimentation' as one of the titles. What does experimentation mean to you?
Provide information to staff about the survey scale. Answering *'Neutral'* in a survey questionnaire is calculated as a negative response. Differentiate between *'Not Applicable'* and *'Neutral'*

Annexure 5.5

Go See Learn: Sample Conversation Starter Questions – Worklife Pulse
How are job routines and expectations shared with you?   Explain what your typical day looks like.   In what way do you get informed about changes in your area?   What does creative problem solving mean to you? Does your job routine allow you the opportunity for creative problem solving?   What are some of your skills that you have not had the opportunity to use in the workplace?   What are some of the challenges that hinder your job productivity?   How do you use the celebration section of the Huddle Board?   When was the last time you were recognized?   How often do you recognize others for the work they do?
Is there any specific training need identified that will help you in your job?   How does your learning plan align with your professional growth?
What does respect look like to you?   Do you ask for help from your team? Tell me more...   How do you orient a new team member in your area?   How often do you recognize others for the work they do?
What does respect look like to you?   How do you like to receive feedback?   What support do you need from me?   What would improve the RDR experience for you?
How might Senior Management communicate more effectively with you?   How might Senior Management demonstrate their commitment to quality of care?   How might Senior Management show that your feedback matters?
Share your ideas on how Senior Management could bridge the gap between organization priorities and your team's priorities?   How has the realignment of our services and organizational changes supported you in providing quality healthcare?   How have the huddle boards affected implementation and escalation of your suggestions?   Provide some suggestions to improve the health and safety in your work environment?
What are your strategies to prevent violence or abuse in the workplace?   Could you suggest a few ideas to prevent violence or abuse in the workplace?   Do you feel safe at work? Tell me more...   What would your family say about your work/life balance?   What is your personal strategy to manage stress at work?
Tell me about a time you were proud of the work you and your team did?   What is the best thing you would share with your family about your work at the hospital?   What motivates you at work?   What is one thing you would like to change in your area?   Are people achieving their best?   What do you do to improve your workplace experience?   Is there is anything we could do to help improve your workplace experience?
Provide information to staff about the survey scale. Answering '*Neutral*' in a survey questionnaire is calculated as a negative response. Differentiate between '*Not Applicable*' and '*Neutral*'

Annexure 5.6

Go See Learn: Conversation Starters Associated with Accreditation Themes on Patient Safety				
	SURVEY QUESTIONS	**CONVERSATION STARTERS**	**Red**	**Yellow**
Organizational leadership support for safety	Patient safety decisions are made at the proper level by the most qualified people.	What is the process of addressing a safety issue in your area?		
	Senior management has a clear picture of the risk associated with patient care.	Help me better understand the challenges you face on a daily basis?		
	Senior management provides a climate that promotes patient safety.	Tell me more about some of the challenges you face regarding patient safety...		
	Senior management considers patient safety when program changes are discussed.	Share some of your ideas to improve patient safety in your area.		
	My organization effectively balances the need for patient safety and the need for productivity.	What are staff and leaders at all levels doing well to promote a patient safety climate, and what can we do better? How can we ensure patient safety is considered in all decisions? When you are having a busy day, how do you continue to deliver high quality, safe care?		
Supervisory leadership for safety	My supervisor/manager says a good word when he/she sees a job done according to established patient safety procedures.	How do you like to be recognized? How could we promote good catches in our area?		
	My supervisor/manager seriously considers staff suggestions for improving patient safety.	Is there a process for bringing forward safety ideas in your area? Share some of your ideas to improve patient safety in our area.		
Unit Learning culture	On this unit, when a serious error occurs, we think about it carefully.			
	In my area of care, after a serious error has occurred, we think about how it came about and how to prevent the same mistake in the future.	Think of an incident that occurred in your area. How would you prevent the same mistake in the future?		
	On this unit, when a serious error occurs, we analyze it thoroughly.			
	On this unit, after a serious error has occurred, we think long and hard about how to correct it.			

(*Continued*)

Incident follow-up	Individuals involved in patient safety incidents have a quick and easy way to report what happened.	What type of incidents would you typically report in REDS? Are there any safety issues that you have reported and have not yet been addressed? What is the process when you witness or learn about an incident?		
	If I report a patient safety incident, someone usually follows up to get more information from me.			
	If I point out a potentially serious patient safety incident, management will look into it.			
	Staff are usually given feedback about changes put into place based on incident reports.			
Enabling open communication: judgment free environment	If I make a serious error my manager will think I am incompetent.	How might we make it safe to discuss errors? Tell me how I could help you overcome your fear of experimentation. The huddles boards have 'Experimentation' as one of the titles. What does experimentation mean to you?		
	My coworkers will lose respect for me if they know I've made a serious error.			
	Others make you feel like a bit of a failure when you make an error.			
Enabling open communication: job repercussions of error	Making a serious error may cause a staff member to lose his/her job.			
	If I make a serious error I worry that I will face disciplinary action from management.			
	If I make a serious error it will limit my career opportunities around here.			
	Survey Likert Scale	Provide information to staff about the survey scale. Answering 'Neutral' in a survey questionnaire is calculated as a negative response. Differentiate between 'Not Applicable' and 'Neutral'		

Annexure 5.7

Go See Learn: Conversation Starters Associated with Accreditation Themes on Worklife Pulse				
	SURVEY STATEMENTS	CONVERSATION STARTERS	Red	Yellow
Your Job	I understand what is expected of me in my job.	How are job routines and expectations shared with you?		
	I am given enough time to do what is expected of me in my job.	Explain what your typical day looks like.		
	I am consulted about changes affecting my job.	In what way do you get informed about changes in your area?		
	I am able to decide how to do my work.	What does creative problem solving mean to you? Does your job routine allow you the opportunity for creative problem solving?		
	I am able to make improvements in how my work is done.			
	My job makes good use of my skills.	What are some of your skills that you have not had the opportunity to use in the workplace?		
	I have the materials, supplies, and equipment I need to do my work.	What are some of the challenges that hinder your job productivity?		
	I receive recognition for good work.	How do you use the celebration section of the Huddle Board? When was the last time you were recognized? How often do you recognize others for the work they do?		
Training & Development	I receive the training I need to do my job well.	Is there any specific training need identified that will help you in your job?		
	I have good opportunities to develop my career.	How does your learning plan align with your professional growth?		
Your Coworkers	The people I work with treat me with respect.	What does respect look like to you?		
	The people I work with help each other out.	Do you ask for help from your team? Tell me more...		
	I feel I belong to a team	How do you orient a new team member in your area? How often do you recognize others for the work they do?		
Your Immediate Supervisor	My supervisor treats me fairly.	What does respect look like to you?		
	My supervisor provides feedback on how well I am doing my job.	How do you like to receive feedback?		
	I can count on my supervisor to help me with a difficult task.	What support do you need from me? What would improve the RDR experience for you?		

(*Continued*)

		How might Senior Management communicate more effectively with you?		
The Organizations Senior Management	Senior managers effectively communicate the organization's goals.	How might Senior Management demonstrate their commitment to quality of care?		
	Senior managers are committed to providing high-quality care.	How might Senior Management show that your feedback matters?		
		Share your ideas on how Senior Management could bridge the gap between organization priorities and your team's priorities.		
	Senior managers act on staff feedback.	How has the realignment of our services and organizational changes supported you in providing quality healthcare?		
	Senior managers are committed to providing a safe and healthy workplace.	How have the Huddle Boards affected implementation and escalation of your suggestions?		
		Provide some suggestions to improve the health and safety in your work environment?		
Safety & Health	My organization takes effective action to prevent violence in the workplace.	What are your strategies to prevent violence or abuse in the workplace?		
	My organization takes effective action to prevent abuse in the workplace.	Could you suggest a few ideas to prevent violence or abuse in the workplace?		
	My workplace is safe.	Do you feel safe at work? Tell me more...		
	I am able to balance my family and personal life with work.	What would your family say about your work/life balance?		
	In the past 12 months, would you say that most days at work were stressful?	What is your personal strategy to manage stress at work?		
Your Overall Experience	How often does your work team provide top-quality patient care or other services?	Tell me about a time you were proud of the work you and your team did?		
		What is the best thing you would share with your family about your work at the hospital?		
	Would you recommend this organization to friends and family who require care?	What motivates you at work?		
	How frequently do you look forward to going to work?	What is one thing you would like to change in your area?		
	Overall, how satisfied are you with your job?	Are people achieving their best?		
		What do you do to improve your workplace experience?		
	Overall, how would you rate your organization as a place to work?	Is there is anything we could do to help improve your workplace experience?		
	Survey Likert Scale	Provide information to staff about the survey scale. Answering 'Neutral' in a survey questionnaire is calculated as a negative response. Differentiate between 'Not Applicable' and 'Neutral'		

Annexure 6

Standard Work for Manager Daily Status			
Last Updated:		**Performed By:**	Managers
Revision:		**Frequency:**	Daily
Standard Work Owner:	Managers	**Duration:**	15 minutes

Standard Work Purpose: The purpose of the Daily Status Sheet is for the leader to meet with their team leads/ supervisors/ coordinators to recognize trends early, act on them as needed, and also understand the developmental and coaching needs of staff. This is a problem–solving tool for proactive planning for the day that supports quality initiatives, and promotes the values and strategic directions of Hospital Heal.

PLAN

1. Prepare Daily Status Sheet

Manager obtains Daily Status Sheet, pre-populated with organization-wide mandatory questions. Manager with the team lead/supervisor/coordinator have an option to create and add team-specific questions that will help you know what is happening in your area(s). Do not exceed a total of 12 questions.

2. Schedule Daily Status Conversation

Manager and team lead/supervisor/coordinator set an established, agreed upon time and place to have the daily status conversation.

DO

3. Complete Daily Status Sheet Together

Manager and team lead/supervisor/coordinator meet at predetermined time every day from Monday to Friday, in a space conducive to uninterrupted conversation and feedback, and complete the Daily Status Sheet together.
- *Ask the questions and ONLY record actionable items for follow up*
- *Fill in the visual indicator   with a **green** marker, if plan in place does not impact the question negatively*
- *Fill in the visual indicator   with a **red** marker, if there is no plan in place or the plan impacts the question negatively*
- *Follow up on any pending issues from the previous Daily Status Sheets*
- *Record any ideas that require team consensus on 'Ideas/How might we...?' cards and bring to the next Huddle. Encourage staff to experiment*

4. Complete Weekly Overview on Thursday

Every Thursday, during the Daily Status conversation, manager and team leader/supervisor/coordinator complete the weekly overview questions.
Follow up on any pending issues from the previous Weekly Status Sheet section.

STUDY

5. Analyze the Data

Manager reviews and analyzes the data collected through the Daily Status Sheet and shares any relevant information during the Director's Weekly Status conversation.
Manager incorporates relevant information into the Monthly Scorecard Review.

ADJUST

Through experimentation, your leadership team and staff will begin to influence your Status Sheet.

Annexure 6.1

Manager Daily Status Sheet			
Name:		Manager:	
Unit/Area name:		Date:	

	Conversation Questions	Mon	Tues	Wed	Thur	Fri	Actionable Items
Access to the Right Care	What is a potential quality or safety issue today?	○	○	○	○	○	**Monday**
	What could interrupt your work flow and/or your team's work flow today?	○	○	○	○	○	
		○	○	○	○	○	
		○	○	○	○	○	**Tuesday**
Partnerships with Purpose	How will your team's work impact other areas today?	○	○	○	○	○	
	How will other areas/departments impact your team's work today?	○	○	○	○	○	
		○	○	○	○	○	**Wednesday**
Our People Achieving their Best	What improvement(s) are we working on today?	○	○	○	○	○	
	Who or what should we celebrate or recognize today?	○	○	○	○	○	
	Who is going to need the most support today and what is your plan?	○	○	○	○	○	**Thursday**
	What courageous conversations will you have today?	○	○	○	○	○	
		○	○	○	○	○	
Wise Choices	What could positively or negatively impact our budget today?	○	○	○	○	○	**Friday**
	What is your priority today and how can I help you?	○	○	○	○	○	
		○	○	○	○	○	

(Continued)

Weekly overview questions

What trends are you seeing this week?	⬤	
What did you learn about your business/area this week?	⬤	
How will your team include patient/family and customer voice in projects/initiatives/Just Do Its this week?	⬤	
What challenges are you anticipating in your Huddles this week?	⬤	
What could potentially contribute to injuries and absenteeism, and how are you addressing them?	⬤	
How might we engage external partners to improve patient experience this week?	⬤	

Optional Questions

How might we engage internal partners to improve patient experience?	How might we utilize Volunteer Services in your area this week?
Are there any Recognition and Development Reviews that need to be completed this week?	Who will you coach this week, and how do you anticipate they'll respond?

Annexure 7

Standard Work for Director Daily Status			
Last Updated:		**Performed By:**	Directors
Revision:		**Frequency:**	Weekly per area
Standard Work Owner:	Directors	**Duration:**	15 minutes

Standard Work Purpose: The purpose of the Director Weekly Status Sheet is for the leader to meet with their managers to recognize trends early, act on them as needed, and also understand the developmental and coaching needs of staff. This is a problem solving tool for proactive planning for the day that supports quality initiatives, and promotes the values and strategic directions of Hospital Heal.

PLAN

1. Prepare Weekly Status Sheet

Director obtains a Weekly Status Sheet, pre-populated with organization-wide mandatory questions. Director with the Manager have an option to create and add team-specific questions that will help you know what is happening in your area(s) weekly. Do not exceed a total of 12 questions.

2. Schedule Weekly Status Conversation

Director and Manager set an established, agreed upon time and place to have the Weekly Status conversation.

DO

3. Complete Weekly Status Sheet Together

Director and Manager meet at predetermined time weekly, in a space conducive to uninterrupted conversation and feedback, and complete the Weekly Status Sheet together.
- *Ask the questions and record anticipated concerns or issues that are outside the control of the Manager on the Weekly Status Sheet.*
- *Fill in the visual indicator with a **green** marker to indicate action taken.*
- *Fill in the visual indicator with a **red** marker to indicate action required.*
- *Record any ideas that require team consensus on 'Ideas/How might we...?' cards and the Manager will bring to the next Huddle.*
- *Follow up on any pending issues from the previous Weekly Status Sheets.*

STUDY

4. Analyze the Data

Director reviews and analyzes the data collected through the Weekly Status conversation and provides relevant information to the Manager for the Monthly Scorecard Review.

ADJUST

Through experimentation, your leadership team and staff will begin to influence your Status Sheet.

Annexure 7.1

Director Weekly Status Sheet							
Name:				**Director:**			
Unit/Area name:				**Date:**			

	Conversation Questions	Mon	Tues	Wed	Thur	Fri	Actionable Items
Access to the Right Care	What is a potential quality or safety issue this week?	●	●	●	●	●	**Monday**
	What could interrupt your work flow this week?	●	●	●	●	●	
	How will your team include patient/family/customer voice in projects/initiatives/Just Do Its this week?	●	●	●	●	●	
		●	●	●	●	●	**Tuesday**
Partnerships with Purpose	How might we engage external partners to improve patient experience?	●	●	●	●	●	
	How will other areas/departments impact your teams' work this week?	●	●	●	●	●	
		●	●	●	●	●	**Wednesday**
Our People Achieving their Best	What improvement(s) are we working on this week?	●	●	●	●	●	
	Who or what should we celebrate or recognize this week?	●	●	●	●	●	
	Are there any Recognition and Development Reviews that you need to complete this week?	●	●	●	●	●	**Thursday**
	What courageous conversations will you have this week?	●	●	●	●	●	
		●	●	●	●	●	
Wise Choices	What could positively or negatively impact our budget this week?	●	●	●	●	●	**Friday**
	What is your priority this week and how can I help you?	●	●	●	●	●	
		●	●	●	●	●	

Optional Questions	
What trends are you seeing this week?	How might we utilize Volunteer Services in your area this week?
What did you learn about your business/area this week?	What challenges are you anticipating in your Huddles this week?
What do you see happening in the next week/month/ quarter that will affect your department/team?	Who will you coach this week, and how do you anticipate they'll respond?
How might we engage internal partners to improve patient experience?	

Annexure 8

Standard Work for Monthly Performance Scorecard Review			
Last Updated:		**Performed By:**	Manager/Director/VP
Revision:		**Frequency:**	Once a month, on the 3rd or 4th week of the month
Standard Work Owner:	Manager/Director	**Meeting Duration:**	60–180 minutes

Standard Work Purpose: To have the Managers, Directors and Vice President reflect as a team on the performance of the scorecard metrics that are aligned to the organization's Strategic Directions. To create a supportive environment that encourages experimentation; share lessons learned; identify opportunities for improvement; overcome barriers and create value through partnerships.

PLAN

- Complete the Template for the Monthly Performance Scorecard Review.
- Enter all the scorecard data for the previous month in your template. Color your metrics (RED, YELLOW, GREEN) to reflect the monthly performance. Note: In all metrics other than financial budget, more than 10% variation from target is Red and between 0.1 to 10% is Yellow. For financial budget metric, more than 1% deviation from target is Red and between 0.1 to 1% is Yellow.
- For each RED and YELLOW metric prepare responses to the following three questions:
  a. What's working well?
  b. What's not working well?
  c. What support do you need?

Monthly Performance Scorecard Review Guidelines

Tone:
- Supportive, safe environment to share information
- Shared accountability
- Promote sense of urgency

Assumptions:
- Scorecard metric data is updated and current
- Presenters will follow standard work
- Conversation focuses not on barriers but on: *"How might we...?"*

What to consider when problem-solving:
- Root cause analysis vs. firefighting
- Go see learn
- Respect for people
- Creativity before capital
- Experiment before abandoning any idea
- Avoid postponed perfection
- The bias is for action: learn by doing

DO

1. Welcome Team

The VP welcomes the Team and Guests to Monthly Scorecard Review. The Director or Manager presents the scorecard.

2. The Presenter Shares the Performance Scorecard Metrics (maximum 15 minutes)

- Highlight overall performance of the scorecard
- Start with a positive note by Celebrating the GREEN metric(s)
- The Director supports the Manager in answering questions. For each RED and YELLOW metric focus on the following three questions:
  a. What's working well?
  b. What's not working well?
  c. What support do you need?
- Record Commitments, To Do's and team Reflections from the meeting

STUDY

Manager, Director and Senior Leader share and discuss their learnings at the Huddle with your team.

ADJUST

Through experimentation your learnings will influence your next Monthly Scorecard Review.

Annexure 8.1

Standard Work Template for Monthly Performance Scorecard review

ACCESS TO THE RIGHT CARE			
			June '14
Metric	Tar	Act	Var
% preventative maintenance procedures met in compliance with best practice guideline for ECRI and risk classification priority one	90%	36%	54%
% preventative maintenance procedures met in compliance with best practice guideline for ECRI and risk classification priority two	60%	50%	10%
% preventative maintenance procedures met in compliance with best practice guideline for ECRI and risk classification priority three	30%	30%	0%

OUR PEOPLE ACHIEVING THEIR BEST			
			June '14
Metric	Tar	Act	Var
% Staff Recognition & Development Reviews Completed for those eligible	100%	0	100%
Total number of staff injuries/illnesses reported to WSIB	0	0	0
Average paid illness days per employee	≤ 10.23	0	0

PARTNERSHIP WITH PURPOSE			
			June '14
Metric	Tar	Act	Var
Number of biotech and/or IT student placements completed	1	1	0

WISE CHOICES			
			June '14
Metric	Tar	Act	Var
Budget Variance %	≤ 0%	0.9%	0.9%

Annexure 9

Standard Work for Visual Room Performance Review			
Last Updated:		**Performed By:**	Senior Leadership Team
Revision:		**Frequency:**	As scheduled
Standard Work Owner:	CEO	**Duration:**	60–90 minutes

Standard Work Purpose: The Visual Room Performance Review provides an opportunity for the Senior Leadership Team to visualize and evaluate performance, understand problems, provide necessary support, implement responses, and celebrate experiments. The Visual Room is where the CEO and the Vice Presidents gather regularly to strategize and reflect as a team on the performance of the organization.

PLAN

Ensure the Visual Room data is populated and up to date. Prepare to speak to yellow and red metrics. Post any celebrations and support requests.

DO

1. Welcome Team and Guests

2. Review Organization Report Card

Provide a high-level overview of the Organization Report Card, identifying metrics that are RED and YELLOW and celebrating metrics that are GREEN.

3. Review Service Level Metrics and Associated Projects

Each Vice President reviews their Service Level metrics and projects.

For each RED and YELLOW metric focus on the following:

- What's working well?
- What's not working well?
- What support do you need?

Link the metrics to the corresponding projects, Build Foundations For, How Can We Help and Celebrations.

Highlight projects/initiatives that are impacted by resource constraints.

4. Review How Can We Help?

Review any support requests. This is an opportunity to ask the team for any ideas or suggestions to assist with overcoming a problem or barrier to meet targets.

5. Celebrate

End on a high note: Review and celebrate projects implemented, accomplishments, thank you notes, good news, and patient/staff compliments. Identify what teams and individuals should receive a special recognition (thank you note).

STUDY

Reflect on the areas of focus and their alignment to the organization Report Card. Brainstorm How Might We…? improve organization performance.

ADJUST

Bring considerations back to the Directors' group to confirm organization priorities. Implement countermeasures, as appropriate. Follow up with the respective teams on their support requests.

Through experimentation, your learnings will influence the next Visual Room Performance Review.

Annexure 10

STANDARD FACILITATION KIT SIGN OUT SHEET

Name (Please Print)	Kit Number	Date Out	Date In	Restocked upon return?
	① ② ③ ④ ⑤			☐ Yes ☐ No
	① ② ③ ④ ⑤			☐ Yes ☐ No
	① ② ③ ④ ⑤			☐ Yes ☐ No
	① ② ③ ④ ⑤			☐ Yes ☐ No
	① ② ③ ④ ⑤			☐ Yes ☐ No
	① ② ③ ④ ⑤			☐ Yes ☐ No
	① ② ③ ④ ⑤			☐ Yes ☐ No
	① ② ③ ④ ⑤			☐ Yes ☐ No
	① ② ③ ④ ⑤			☐ Yes ☐ No
	① ② ③ ④ ⑤			☐ Yes ☐ No
	① ② ③ ④ ⑤			☐ Yes ☐ No
	① ② ③ ④ ⑤			☐ Yes ☐ No
	① ② ③ ④ ⑤			☐ Yes ☐ No
	① ② ③ ④ ⑤			☐ Yes ☐ No
	① ② ③ ④ ⑤			☐ Yes ☐ No

Bibliography

1. Anderson, L.A. and D. Anderson. *The Change Leader's Roadmap—How to Navigate your Organization's Transformation*. San Francisco: Pfeiffer, 2008.
2. Axelrod, R. *Terms of Engagement: New Ways of Leading and Changing Organizations*. San Francisco: Berrett-Koehler, 2010.
3. Ballard, D.J. *Achieving STEEEP Healthcare*. Boca Raton, FL: CRC Press, 2014.
4. Balle, M. *The Gold Mine*. Cambridge, MA: Lean Enterprise Institute, 2005.
5. Barnas, K. *Beyond Heroes: A Lean Management System for Healthcare*. Appleton, WI: ThedaCare Center for Healthcare Value, 2014.
6. Basadur, M. *The Power of Innovation*. Toronto, Ontario, Canada: Applied Creativity Press, 2001.
7. Behavioural Descriptors supporting the College CHETM Program—LEADS in a Caring Environment Framework—June 2011.
8. Black, J. and D. Miller. *The Toyota Way to Healthcare Excellence*. Chicago, IL: Health Administration Press, 2008.
9. Blanchard, K. *Gung Ho! Turn On the People in Any Organization*. New York, NY: William Morrow, 1997.
10. Block, P. *The Empowered Manager: Positive Political Skills at Work*. San Francisco: Jossey-Bass/Pfeiffer, 1987.
11. Bono, E. De. *Lateral Thinking: Creativity Step by Step*. New York, NY: Harper Colophon, 2015.
12. Bossidy, L. and R. Charan. *Confronting Reality*. London, UK: Random House Business Books, 2004.
13. Braksick, L.W. *Unlock Behavior Unleash Profits: Developing Leadership Behavior that Drives Profitability in Your Organization*. New York, NY: McGraw-Hill, 2007.
14. Bridges, W. *Transitions: Making Sense of Life's Changes*. Reading, MA: Addison-Wesley Publishing, 2004.
15. Buckingham, M. and C. Coffman. *First Break All the Rules*. New York, NY: Simon & Schuster, 1999.
16. Cameron, K.S. and R.E. Quinn. *Diagnosing and Changing Organizational Culture: Based on the Competing Values Framework*. San Francisco: Jossey-Bass, 2010.

17. Cameron, K. An Introduction to the Competing Values Framework. http://faculty.mu.edu.sa/public/uploads/1360773197.1216organizational%20cult125.pdf

18. Christensen C.M., S.D. Anthony, and E.A. Roth. *Seeing What's Next.* Boston, MA: Harvard Business Publishing, 2004.

19. Clark, K.B., C.Y. Baldwin, J. Magretta, J.H. Dyer, and M.L. Fisher. *Harvard Business Review on Managing the Value Chain.* Boston, MA: Harvard Business School Press, 2000.

20. Cobb, C.G. *From Quality to Business Excellence: A Systems Approach to Management.* Milwaukee, WI: ASQ Quality Press, 2003.

21. Collins, J. and J.I. Porras. *Built to Last: Successful Habits of Visionary Companies.* New York, NY: HarperBusiness, 2004.

22. Collins, J. *Good to Great: Why Some Companies Make the Leap ... and Others Don't.* New York, NY: HarperCollins, 2001.

23. Cook, R. and A. Jenkins. *Building a Problem-Solving Culture that Lasts.* McKinsey & Company, 2014, http://www.mckinsey.com/~/media/McKinsey/Business%20Functions/Operations/Our%20Insights/The%20lean%20management%20enterprise/Building%20a%20problem%20solving%20culture%20that%20lasts.ashx

24. Covey, S. *7 Habits of Highly Effective People: Powerful Lessons in Personal Change.* New York, NY: Simon & Schuster, 1989.

25. Dickson, G. and B. Tholl. *Bringing Leadership to Life in Health: LEADS in a Caring Environment.* London: Springer, 2014.

26. Eaton, D. and G. Kilby. Does your organizational culture support your business strategy? *Journal for Quality and 4 Participation,* January 2015.

27. Dr. Goldsmith, Marshall. *Mojo: How to Get It, How to Keep It, How to Get It Back If You Lose It.* New York, NY: Hachette Books, 2010.

28. Dr. Goldsmith, Marshall. *What Got You Here Won't Get You There.* New York, NY: Hachette Books, 2007.

29. European Foundation for Quality Management, www.efqm.org

30. Evans, J. and S. Chuck. *Ten Tasks of Change: Demystifying Changing Organizations.* San Francisco: Jossey-Bass/Pfeiffer, 2001.

31. Farson, R. *Management of the Absurd: Paradoxes in Leadership.* New York, NY: Touchstone, 1996.

32. Ferrazzi, K. *Never Eat Alone.* New York, NY: Doubleday, 2005.

33. Friedman, T. *The World is Flat: A Brief History of the Twenty-First Century.* New York, NY: Picador, 2007.

34. George, M.L. *Lean Six Sigma for Service.* New Delhi, India: Tata McGraw-Hill, 2003.

35. Girard, J.P. and J.L. Girard. Defining knowledge management: Toward an applied compendium. *Online Journal of Applied Knowledge Management,* 2015.

36. Gladwell, M. *Outliers: The Story of Success.* New York, NY: Back Bay Books, 2011.

37. Gladwell, M. *The Tipping Point.* New York, NY: Little, Brown and Company, 2000.

38. Goldratt, E.M. *Critical Chain*. MA: North River Press, 2002.
39. Goldratt, E.M. *It's Not Luck*. MA: North River Press, 1994.
40. Goldratt, E.M. *The Goal: A Process of Ongoing Improvement*. MA: North River Press, 2014.
41. Goleman D. Leadership that gets results. *Harvard Business Review*, 2000.
42. Goleman, D. *Working with Emotional Intelligence*. New York, NY: Bantam Doubleday Dell, 1998.
43. Goran, J., L. LaBerge, and R. Srinivasan. Culture for digital age. *McKinsey Quarterly*, July 17, http://www.mckinsey.com/business-functions/digital-mckinsey/our-insights/culture-for-a-digital-age
44. Graban, M. *Lean Hospitals: Improving Quality, Patient Safety, and Employee Engagement*. New York, NY: Productivity Press, 2011.
45. Greif, M. *The Visual Factory*. CT: Productivity Press, 1989.
46. Halvorson, G.C. The culture to cultivate. *HBR* issue July–August 2013, https://hbr.org/2013/07/the-culture-to-cultivate
47. Hamel, G. and C.K. Prahalad. *Competing for the Future*. Boston, MA: Harvard Business Review Press, 1996.
48. Hammer, M. and J.A. Champy. *Reengineering the Corporation: A Manifesto for Business Revolution*. Australia: HarperBusiness, 2006.
49. Harris, R., C. Harris, and E. Wilson. *Making Materials Flow*. MA: LEI, 2003.
50. Harvey, J. *Managing Service Delivery Processes: Linking Strategy to Operations*. Milwaukee, WI: ASQ Quality Press, 2006.
51. Heath, D. and C. Heath. *Made to Stick*. New York, NY: Random House, 2007.
52. Heath, D. and C. Heath. *Switch: How to Change Things When Change Is Hard*. New York, NY: Crown Business, 2010.
53. Heifetz, R.A. *Leadership Without Easy Answers*. Cambridge, MA: Belknap Press, 1994.
54. Hirano, H. *Putting 5S to Work*. New York, NY: PHP Institute, 1993.
55. http://www.kornferry.com/institute/real-world-leadership-part-three-create-an-engaging-culture-for-greater-impact
56. Imai, M. *Gemba Kaizen*. New York, NY: McGraw-Hill, 1997.
57. Imai, M. *Gemba Kaizen: A Commonsense Approach to a Continuous Improvement Strategy*. New York, NY: McGraw-Hill Education, 2012.
58. Johnson, S. *Who Moved my Cheese? New York, NY: G.P.* Putnam's Sons, 1998.
59. Katzenbach, J. and A. de Aguirre. Culture and the Chief Executive. Strategy & Summer 2013/Issue 71, https://www.strategy-business.com/article/00179?gko=6912e
60. Kaplan, R.S. and D.P. Norton. *Strategy Maps: Converting Intangible Assets into Intangible Outcomes*. Boston, MA: Harvard Business School Publishing, 2004.
61. Kaplan, R.S. and D.P. Norton. *The Balanced Scorecard: Translating Strategy into Action*. Boston, MA: Harvard Business School Press, 1996.
62. Kellerman, B. *The End of Leadership*. New York, NY: HarperCollins, 2012.
63. King's Fund. *The Future of Leadership and Management in the NHS: No More Heroes*. London: The Kings Fund, 2011.

64. Kotter, J.P. and D.S. Cohen. *The Heart of Change: Real-Life Stories of How People Change Their Organizations.* Boston, MA: Harvard Business School Press, 2002.

65. Kotter, J. and H. Rathgeber. *Our Iceberg is Melting.* New York, NY: St. Martin's Press, 2005.

66. Kotter, J. *Leading Change.* Boston, MA: Harvard Business School Press, 1996.

67. Kouzes, J.M. and B.Z. Posner. *Encouraging the Heart: A Leader's Guide to Rewarding and Recognizing Others.* New York, NY: Simon & Schuster, 2007.

68. Lencioini, P.M. *The Five Dysfunctions of a Team: A Leadership Fable.* San Francisco: Jossey-Bass, 2002.

69. Liker, J. *The Toyota Way: 14 Management Principles from the World's Greatest Manufacturer.* New Delhi, India: Tata McGraw-Hill, 2004.

70. Liker, J.K. and H. Michael. *Toyota Culture: The Heart and Soul of the Toyota Way.* New Delhi, India: Tata McGraw-Hill, 2008.

71. Loehr, J. and T. Schwartz. *The Power of Full Engagement: Managing Energy, Not Time, is the Key to High Performance and Personal Renewal.* Free Press, 2003.

72. Malcolm B. www.quality.nist.gov

73. Mann, D. *Creating a Lean Culture: Tools to Sustain Lean Conversations.* Boca Raton, FL: CRC Press, 2005.

74. McGoff, C. *The Primes: How Any Group Can Solve Any Problem.* New York, NY: Victory Publishers, 2011.

75. Merrill, P. *Innovation Generation: Creating an Innovation Process and an Innovative Culture.* Milwaukee, WI: ASQ Quality Press, 2008.

76. Nakamuro, J. Re-Translating Lean from Its Origin, Jan 17, https://www.linkedin.com/pulse/re-translating-lean-from-its-origin-jun-nakamuro

77. Niven, P.R. *Balanced Scorecard Step-by-Step: Maximizing Performance and Maintaining Results.* New York, NY: John Wiley & Sons, 2002.

78. *Operational Excellence in 2017.* Senior Executives Insights, PEX Network.

79. Patterson, K., J. Grenny, R. McMillan, and A. Switzler. *Crucial Conversations: Tools for Talking when Stakes are High.* New York, NY: McGraw-Hill, 2012.

80. Perlo, J., B. Balik, S. Swensen, A. Kabcenell, J. Landsman, and D. Feeley. *IHI Framework for Improving Joy in Work.* IHI White Paper. Cambridge, MA: Institute for Healthcare Improvement, 2017. (Available at ihi.org)

81. Peters, T. *The Circle of Innovation: You Can't Shrink Your Way to Greatness.* New York, NY: Vintage Books, 1999.

82. Pointer, D.D. and J.E. Orlikoff. *Board Work: Governing Healthcare Organizations.* New York, NY: John Wiley and Sons, 1999.

83. Quinn, R.E. *Deep Change: Discovering the Leader Within.* San Francisco: Jossey-Bass, 1996.

84. Rother, M. and R. Harris. *Creating Continuous Flow.* Cambridge, MA: LEI, 2001.

85. Rother, M. and J. Shook. *Learning to See.* MA: LEI, 1998.

86. Rother, M. *Toyota Kata: Managing People for Improvement, Adaptiveness and Superior Results.* New York, NY: McGraw-Hill Education, 2009.

87. SAI Global, www.sai-global.com

88. Schultz, H. *Onward: How Starbucks Fought for Its Life without Losing Its Soul.* New York, NY: Rodale Books, 2012.

89. Schwarz, R. *The Skilled Facilitator.* San Francisco: Jossey-Bass, 2002.

90. Sekine, K. and K. Arai. *Kaizen for Quick Changeover.* Portland, OR: Productivity Press, 1987.

91. Senge, P.M. *The Fifth Discipline: The Art and Practice of the Learning Organization.* London: Random House, 1990.

92. Senge, P. *The Dance of Change.* New York, NY: Doubleday, 2002.

93. Senge, P. *The Fifth Discipline: The Art and Practice of a Learning Organization.* New York, NY: Doubleday, 2002.

94. Sharma, R. *The Monk Who Sold His Ferrari.* New York, NY: HarperCollins, 1998.

95. Shook, J. *Managing to Learn: Using the A3 Management Process.* Cambridge, MA: LEI, 2008.

96. Silverstein, D., N. DeCarlo, and S. Michael. *Insourcing Innovation: How to Transform Business as Usual into Business as Exceptional.* Longmont, CO: Breakthrough Performance Press, 2005.

97. Silverstein, D., P. Samuel, and N. DeCarlo. *The Innovator's Toolkit: 50+ Techniques for Predictable and Sustainable Organic Growth.* Hoboken, NJ: John Wiley & Sons, 2009.

98. Smalley, A. *Creating Level Pull.* Brookline, MA: LEI, 2004.

99. Sperl, T., R. Ptacek, and J. Trewn. *Practical Lean Six Sigma for Healthcare.* Chelsea, MI: MCS Media Inc, 2013.

100. SRL, Ernest and Young. Using tollgate to manage your projects in action. *Business Digest,* Oct'13, http://rbd.doingbusiness.ro/news/using-tollgates-to-manage-your-project-in-action/2504

101. Suzaki, K. *The New Manufacturing Challenge.* New York, NY: The Free Press, 1987.

102. Syed, M. *Bounce: The Myth of Talent and the Power of Practice.* London, UK: Fourth Estate, 2011.

103. Torinus, J. *The Company that Solved Health Care.* Dallas, TX: BenBella Books, 2016.

104. Toussaint, J. *On the Mend: Revolutionizing Healthcare to Save Lives and Transform the Industry.* Cambridge, MA: LEI, 2010.

105. Trautlein, B. *Change Intelligence: Use the Power of CQ to Lead Change That Sticks.* Austin, TX: Greenleaf Book Group Press, 2013.

106. Warrell, M. *Stop Playing Safe: Rethink Risk, Unlock the Power of Courage, Achieve Outstanding Success.* UK: Wrightbooks, 2013.

107. Womack, J.P. and D.T. Jones. *Lean Thinking: Banish Waste and Create Wealth in Your Corporation.* New York, NY: Productivity Press, 2003.

108. Womack, J., D. Jones, and D. Ross. *The Machine that Changed the World.* New York, NY: Harper Perennial, 1990.

109. Zygielbaum, P. *Management Lessons from Oz: Leading from Courage.* North Charleston, SC: CreateSpace Independent Publishing Platform, 2016.
110. Baker, M., I. Taylor, and A. Mitchell. How to improve patient care while saving everyone's time and hospitals' resources. *Making Hospitals Work.* Lean Enterprise Academy Limited, May 2009, p. 168.

Index